"*No Tolerance for Tyrants* is a lucidly wri[tten ...] about the Bible's relevance to modern [...] anti-royal bias is far more widespread in the Bible than scholars have thought, and he brilliantly uses ancient Near Eastern texts to illuminate the biblical polemic even in books like Genesis. [This] book is a wonderful mixture of historical scholarship, perceptive literary analysis, and serious concern to grasp the Bible's message for modern readers. It is biblical theology at its best."

—Stuart Irvine
    Associate Professor of Religious Studies
    Louisiana State University

"Weaving together in an accessible style the fruits of current scholarship with excerpts from democratic writings drawing upon the Bible in the 17th and 18th centuries, Gnuse argues convincingly that the biblical critique of kingship is pervasive and revolutionary for its time and ours. Reminding us that many of these texts are so familiar that we cannot see how radical they were, he uncovers the satire, humor, suppressed historical memories, and editorial tweaking that shaped the egalitarian vision of our biblical ancestors in the faith. Surveying biblical texts from the Garden of Eden to the Roman Empire, he calls us to reclaim the Bible as a vehicle of liberation, rather than repression. Like the prophets of old, Gnuse inspires us to look beyond the world's definition of power to the source of that power—God."

—Dr. Denise Dombkowski Hopkins
    Woodrow and Mildred Miller Professor of Biblical Theology
    Wesley Theological Seminary
    Washington, DC

No Tolerance for Tyrants

The Biblical Assault on Kings and Kingship

Robert Gnuse

A Michael Glazier Book

LITURGICAL PRESS
Collegeville, Minnesota

www.litpress.org

A Michael Glazier Book published by Liturgical Press

Cover design by Ann Blattner. Watercolor by Ethel Boyle.

Scripture texts in this work are taken from the *New Revised Standard Version Bible* © 1989, Division of Christian Education of the National Council of the Churches of Christ in the United States of America. Used by permission. All rights reserved.

© 2011 by Order of Saint Benedict, Collegeville, Minnesota. All rights reserved. No part of this book may be reproduced in any form, by print, microfilm, microfiche, mechanical recording, photocopying, translation, or by any other means, known or yet unknown, for any purpose except brief quotations in reviews, without the previous written permission of Liturgical Press, Saint John's Abbey, PO Box 7500, Collegeville, Minnesota 56321-7500. Printed in the United States of America.

1	2	3	4	5	6	7	8

Library of Congress Cataloging-in-Publication Data

Gnuse, Robert Karl, 1947–
    No tolerance for tyrants : the biblical assault on kings and kingship / Robert Gnuse.
        p.   cm.
    "A Michael Glazier book."
    Includes bibliographical references and indexes.
    ISBN 978-0-8146-5762-1 — ISBN 978-0-8146-8007-0 (e-book)
    1. Kings and rulers—Biblical teaching.   I. Title.

BS1199.K5G78   2011
220.8'3216—dc22   2010030952

Contents

Preface

Over the years too many critics outside the church have declared that the Bible is a repressive document. They aver that the Bible justifies war, slavery, the suppression of women, and apathy toward the needs of the poor by affirming authoritarian and patriarchal values and by focusing on spiritual salvation rather than human physical needs. Sadly, many inside the church have abetted these accusations by likewise declaring that Christians should proclaim a message only of spiritual salvation, not social reform. Both groups sadly overlook much of what the Bible actually says about attending to the physical needs of people, and both fail to interpret biblical texts in their social and historical context in order to bring their authentic meaning forth into the modern world.

I have spent my life as a teacher and preacher attempting to tell students and church folk about how the Bible speaks of liberation, not only in the spiritual realm, but also in the physical world—that the Bible speaks of human dignity and equality. I observe that when the Bible is used to justify the suppression of people by slavery, sexism, or economic manipulation, it is abused and its real message thwarted. To that end this book has been written. This book is an attempt to demonstrate how the Bible has inspired the emergence of democratic thought and respect for human equality. The Bible is a powerful source of inspiration when it is interpreted correctly and allowed to speak clearly on human rights. In the past few generations the Roman Catholic Church has wisely drawn on biblical texts to articulate a call for justice in social encyclicals and other ecclesiastical statements. Scholars and Bible professors know full well the message of the Bible on these issues. This textbook is not for the scholars; it is for students—perhaps students who might suspect the Bible to be the source of repression in history and in our modern society.

This book will seek to disabuse them of that notion by highlighting the appropriate texts that affirm human liberation and by recalling those democratic thinkers and politicians in the seventeenth and eighteenth centuries who appealed to the Bible for their political rhetoric.

Scholars too often comment on texts and provide a plethora of interpretative options for various passages in their usual scholarly, technical, objective, fair, dispassionate, and distanced writing styles. I count myself among these scholars; I do the same thing quite often in other writings. But there is a time when one must cut the Gordian knot and boldly declare that ultimately the Bible speaks a powerful message about human equality and dignity, and that as such it has played an important role in the development of our modern democratic values. This book approaches that task by viewing the Bible's perspective on kings and kingship. By expressing criticism of this signal and important human institution, biblical authors were actually affirming the basic equality of all human beings before God more than a thousand years before it became vogue in political discourse. It is a message that needs to be heard again even today, and perhaps the blunt and powerful message of the Bible can proclaim the clarion call that still needs to be sounded.

Thanks are due to folks when books are written and published. I would first like to thank Dave Bossman for permission to reprint two articles from the journal, *Biblical Theology Bulletin*. Chapter 5, "The Moses Traditions," is a revised and lengthened version of "The Assault Upon Kings and Tyrants in the Moses Traditions," *Biblical Theology Bulletin* 39 (2009): 190–203. Chapter 9 is a revised and shortened version of "An Overlooked Message: The Critique of Kings and the Affirmation of Equality in the Primeval History," *Biblical Theology Bulletin* 36 (2006): 46–54. Special thanks go to Hans Christoffersen, Lauren L. Murphy, Mary Stommes, Stephanie Nix, and Colleen Stiller of Liturgical Press for their willingness to publish this work and the patience to undertake the editorial process. Finally, thanks are due to Loyola University for the sabbatical in which I accomplished significant work on the manuscript. May this text open the minds of many students!

Robert Gnuse
New Orleans (Year 5 after the storm)

1. Bible and Political Thinkers

When we speak of kings in the Bible, many images come to mind. We recall stories, such as David's affair with Bathsheba, Absalom's rebellion against David, Solomon's wisdom, Solomon's decision to cut the baby in half, Solomon's meeting with the Queen of Sheba, and Solomon's building the temple. In the New Testament we remember Herod the Great who sought to kill Jesus by slaying all the babies in Bethlehem, or Herod Antipas who beheaded John the Baptist and interviewed Jesus before and after Pilate dealt with him. We recall that Pharaoh in Egypt, who confronted Moses, was also a king. Thus, we have a collection of good and bad memories about royal and regal figures. This would be an accurate reflection of the overall portrayal of kings in the Bible—they did both good and evil. If we read the biblical text from cover to cover, we discover additional stories and statements about kings, mostly negative, especially in the books of 1 and 2 Kings and in the oracles of the prophets. In the books of 1 and 2 Kings we would read of how prophets, particularly Elijah and Elisha, opposed the kings of their age and even were responsible for the ultimate overthrow of two kings who ruled Israel and Judah. The more we read the biblical text, the more we sense deep negative messages about kings and their rule.

Kings in the ancient world, and in Israel, were important to the social, religious, economic, political, and intellectual fabric of society. Students of comparative mythology point out that a great number of myths are told about kings in primitive society as well as the ancient Near East. These myths speak of how kingship arose and why kings were necessary for the harmony and healthy function of society. Indeed, the emergence of kings in the ancient world was necessary for civilization to develop.

Kings organized the life of the community or the territory they ruled in many ways:

1) Kings were the chief leaders of the military in defending the people against foreign conquest. They often were generals, especially in Mesopotamia, or at least they worked closely with generals, as in Egypt. Kings led their nation's armies out in great adventures of conquest to bring back loot or establish trade connections, as was the case with Assyrian and Babylonian empires in the first millennium B.C.E.

2) They often were responsible for collecting and then redistributing food so that everyone was sufficiently fed and the population of the community was sustained. Some rites focused on the king's role in bringing fertility to the crops of the land, especially the New Year's ceremonies in Mesopotamia.

3) In the most ancient well-developed societies of Egypt, Mesopotamia, India, and China, they were responsible for development of irrigation to bring water from rivers to the fields so as to increase crop yield. We call this "agricultural intensification," and some theorists have claimed that this role helped develop strong central government more than anything else in those early civilizations, for the ability to create a well-organized irrigation system required strong political power.

4) Kings proclaimed themselves to be representatives of the gods to the people. Sometimes they were in conflict with the priests over this issue, which resulted in the equivalent of early "church-state" competition, especially in Mesopotamia. We find various texts with different myths advocating the supremacy of the king or the priests. Occasionally the king was the high priest for the community, so there was no conflict. Generally, kings played an important role in determining the will of the divine realm for the world below and for avoiding impurity or divine judgment upon the people. Hittite kings in Turkey especially were concerned with avoiding and eliminating impurity. So kings engaged in appropriate rituals for crop fertility, the avoidance of impurity and evil, and determining the course of action to be taken by society in the political arena.

5) Kings played a significant role in trade. They often coordinated the trade within their own country, for the royal capital was the center to which various goods came and were sent forth to other parts of the country. Even more significantly the kings engaged in international trade, bringing goods from afar that could not otherwise be obtained in the homeland. In Mesopotamia kings were responsible for bringing tin from distant lands, often from Afghanistan, for this element was necessary in the making of bronze tools and weapons. Some Mesopotamian empires arose for the sake of securing tin, and its procurement was a royal monopoly. Mesopotamian kings often controlled the flow of

wood from Phoenicia and Syria into their countries for major building projects. Precious metals and jewels came from afar under royal initiative for both Egyptians and Mesopotamians. Solomon supposedly obtained much of his wealth from trading chariots and horses between Egypt and Asia Minor, and the temple was built primarily with materials brought from foreign lands.

6) Kings were responsible for law and order in society, and they issued law codes to standardize or update law, claiming to have received them directly from a god. Frequently these royal law codes were not really binding on the judges in the law courts, but they were advisory, and they were used to train scribes in the scribal schools, thus performing an educative role upon the intelligentsia and the leaders, which eventually influenced judicial decisions. Kings could function as the final court of appeal, if someone wished to challenge a decision made by elders in the villages (as in Israel) or by judges in more formal courts (as in Egypt or Mesopotamia). But ultimately kings were viewed as the symbols of legal order in society.

7) Kings were a religious and psychological symbol in the minds of the people for the unity and health of the community. Many of the symbols connected to royal regalia and the palace decorations show the king as the symbol for the corporate people. They could describe the king as suffering when they wished to speak about any significant calamity that befell the kingdom. When the king had ill health or was old and impotent, it was believed that the life of the people would be affected by his personal adversity. Biblical texts, too, spoke about the king suffering on behalf of the people of the nation. Jehoiachin's release from a Babylonian prison betokened hope for the eventual release of Jews from Babylonian Exile (2 Kgs 25:27-30).

8) A king could be portrayed as the ultimate symbol of order and wisdom in the land. He was the incarnation of Maʾat, the cosmic principle of wisdom, in Egypt. In Mesopotamia he was the perfect man in terms of courage, wisdom, justice, and power, and he was the steward of the gods. For this reason the king was responsible for providing education for students in the scribal schools. As incarnate divine wisdom, the king functioned as the final court of appeal for all court cases. We are reminded of the story told about Solomon and the two babies in 1 Kgs 3:16-28, wherein he demonstrated wisdom and cleverness in forcing the true mother of the living baby to speak up.

9) Finally, kings could function as priests, even though they usually did not belong to the priestly guild. The king might offer the most important sacrifices, such as those offered by Mesopotamian kings in the New Year festival of Akitu, which ensured that the world would not be destroyed. The pharaoh would

perform the *Sed* festival to restore the power of fertility to the land. Solomon presided over the dedication of the temple (1 Kings 8). Thus, around the personage of the king a web of stories, myth, rituals, and images arose that reflected the fact that he epitomized in his person the life and well-being of the community.[1]

Hence, to criticize the king was a serious matter. But there were times when the king in any society could be criticized, or even overthrown by revolution. That would occur when the particular king in question would fail dramatically in any of the roles described above. We find such language in the ancient world, and it is most clearly articulated by a new king who found it necessary to overthrow his predecessor. Such a "new king," who would found a new dynasty, discovered that it was very necessary to explain how his predecessor had become so totally incompetent, or so insensitive to human suffering in the kingdom, or so completely disaffected from the divine realm, or all of the above, that it was necessary to remove him in order to save society and even the cosmic order. Of course, such language was usually propaganda generated by the regicide upstart, but it was necessary to assuage the concerns of other people in positions of power who might feel that it was dangerous to assault the person of the previous king. The "new king" spent much energy in his royal inscriptions and texts declaring how the gods were unhappy with his predecessor and how the god or gods personally directed him to overthrow his predecessor. We have good examples in inscriptions from a second-millennium B.C.E. Hittite king, Hattushilis III, and a sixth-century B.C.E. Chaldean Babylonian king, Nabonidus, who came to rule by overthrowing the previous kings. One senses the biblical text justified David's succession after Saul with much of the same language in 1 and 2 Samuel.

Given this universal high concern for the importance of kings in the ancient world, it is no wonder that we encounter similar high respect for the king in some of the biblical passages of the Old and New Testaments. That was the value system of the age. What is amazing then, is that we also have so much negative imagery in our biblical text, wherein religious spokespersons criticized kings for their failures in matters of religion or social concern, or brutal and unjust actions, or simply their stupidity. I would maintain that the presence of such narratives in large number has made an impact on the development of political values in Western society, and that this became increasingly the case once literacy and the availability of printed bibles provided greater access to these stories.

II

I must admit there are passages in which kings were described positively. Kings were described as good when they were faithful to Yahweh or advocated the exclusive worship of Yahweh in their kingdoms, for the biblical authors viewed this as the most important criteria by which to judge a king's contributions. One thinks especially of Kings Hezekiah (c. 725–690 B.C.E.) and Josiah (636–609 B.C.E.) in Judah. There was also the vision of the ideal king or messiah who will come someday and establish the age of peace or the golden age. Christians connected this imagery to Jesus, and he became the king par excellence, as well as being priest and prophet for Christians of that time and today. My point is that we should expect such positive imagery, for the institution of kingship was central to the existence of people in the ancient world and they could not have envisioned a society without kings. Nevertheless, the fact that we have so many negative statements and images about kings in the Bible is a telling argument that authors had serious reservations about the nature of kingship.

I believe that there are passages with a strong antiroyal bias that have not been sufficiently noted by commentators in the past. Such negative imagery betokens not just a mere criticism of kings because they have failed in their responsibilities. I believe that within the biblical text there was a deep distrust and disdain for kingship and for tyranny. I suspect that even the positive imagery about good kings, and above all, the hopeful image of the future messiah, were further indictments of the real-life institution of kingship as it was commonly practiced in the ancient world. I believe that unconsciously we have read these texts for the past four hundred years and picked up their ultimate distrust for kings, but we commentators have not consciously noted this.

III

In his thorough analysis of the ideology and social world of kingship in Amorite Babylon, Homeric Greece (whenever that really existed), and ancient Israel, Dale Launderville demonstrates that the institution of kingship was a cultural, social, economic, political, and religious symbol by which societies were unified. Kings held their world together, in part, because of the rhetoric they generated and the economic and political success they could accomplish. They portrayed their rule as sanctioned by the king of the gods, and they helped to mediate the will of the gods to their people, as well as direct the economy, administer the law, and defend the country or city from foreign enemies. I certainly do agree with his analysis. Nonetheless, critique of kingship would occur when kings failed to bring order, basic justice, and prosperity to their society.[2] The biblical critique of kings, especially by the prophets and the Deuteronomistic Historians (the editors of the books of Joshua, Judges, Samuel, and Kings) in ancient Israel, was the most strident we can find in the ancient world. That this critique became enshrined in a sacred text, not edited out, should tell us something about the values of the biblical authors.

What we might not sense is how pervasive that critique is throughout the Bible. Even the portrayal of the ideal king who will come someday criticized kings, for it bespoke a king who will accomplish what living kings do not choose to achieve or simply cannot achieve. Ultimately, Christians connected the image of the messiah with Jesus, who clearly stood in opposition to the institutional kings of this world. The antikingship rhetoric was concomitantly egalitarian, and from that rhetoric democratic ideals arose. It is no coincidence that when the English cut off the head of a ruling monarch in the seventeenth century, they did so while quoting the Bible.[3]

In his very fine work, *Wide as the Waters: The Story of the English Bible and the Revolution It Inspired*, Benson Bobrick declares that the translation of the Bible into the vernacular and its dissemination by the printing press inspired a revolution in England in the seventeenth century on several levels. Once people could read the Bible in their own language and see what it said, they felt encouraged to make their own decisions on the great issues of religion and life in general. The Bible sanctioned the right of people to think for themselves. An open Bible fostered discussion about church authority, which ultimately paved the way for the emergence of constitutional government, which, in turn, evolved into democracy in America. Combined with the new science of astronomy and global exploration, the messages in the Bible began to open the minds of people. In particular, English people became increasingly unhappy with their kings. Selected biblical texts, combined with the Protestant insistence on the universal priesthood of all believers, led them to articulate libertarian ideas. Puritan clergy increased this dissatisfaction by their fiery preaching and their deep self-identification with the prophets of the Hebrew Bible when it came to expressing judgment against the kings of the world. Those who held to the supreme authority of Scripture called for the rights of conscience, free discussion, and an unrestricted press. Thus, the Bible promulgated the belief in the equality of all people.[4] Bobrick is not the first to make such claims, but his book is the latest and a very clear defense of the argument that the Bible laid the foundation for many of our modern assumptions about social justice and human rights. Henning Graf Reventlow traces the concept of biblical authority through the history of English Deism, and among his many observations he notes that the Bible played a very important role in the emergence of Deistic and Enlightenment thought in general, and political theory in particular.[5]

We could go back in time to an earlier translation of the Bible made by John Wycliffe (1330–1384) around 1382. Though literacy was not as great in the fourteenth century as it was in the seventeenth century, when the King James translation appeared, nonetheless, Wycliffe's translation was read by a sufficient number of people to produce significant social movements. Wycliffe himself trained lay preachers who became known as Lollards, and these people were seen later as reformers by some and social dissidents by others. The Lollards advocated the equality of all people before the Gospel. Wycliffe's translation would be condemned at a synod in Oxford in 1408, Wycliffe himself was condemned by the Council of Constance in Italy in 1414, and finally in 1428 his bones were dug up and burned.[6] One of Wycliffe's disciples helped inspire the English Peasants' Revolt of 1381 due to his own close reading of the biblical text.

Not too long after this time the reforms of Jan Hus in Bohemia were inspired by the biblical text. Hus was an ardent admirer of Wycliffe, for Wycliffe's writings were known in Bohemia from 1380 onward. Even though Hus was burned at the stake at the Council of Constance in 1414, his revolutionary movement continued, and a Bohemian reformation occurred from 1415 to 1418. The more radical Hussites established a community at Mount Tabor and surrounding villages, and they articulated beliefs about the total equality of Christians both socially and economically. From 1419 onward they were inspired by biblical texts to emulate the equality of first-century C.E. Christians, and they essentially attempted to become anarcho-communists. Their beliefs brought them in conflict with the Hapsburg Empire and led to their eventual defeat in 1452.[7] Thus, the biblical text helped fuel the fires of some of the peasants' revolts in the Middle Ages.

Some political scientists boldly admit the influence of biblical thought on the development of American democratic ideals, especially biblical texts critical of kingship. Donald Lutz points out that the covenant tradition and other images from the Hebrew Bible influenced important constitutional documents such as the Mayflower Compact (1620), the Pilgrim Code of Law (1636), and the Fundamental Orders of Connecticut (1639), as well as subsequent political documents in the colonies. These documents and other literature were generated by colonial authors deeply indebted to the Calvinist tradition, which in turn, drew heavily on Protestant covenants from religious communities in Europe during the 1500s and 1600s. Equality of all people was justified by appeal to the biblical concept of the image of God. The idea of common law, which protected women, widows, and orphans, was justified by an appeal to passages from the book of Deuteronomy.[8] Biblical imagery and scriptural citations were used by American authors more frequently than citations from Enlightenment thinkers. From 1760 to 1805, 34 percent of citations in political literature came from the Bible compared to only 22 percent for quotes drawn from Enlightenment thinkers, 18 percent from Whig thinkers, 11 percent from common law, 9 percent from classical sources, and 4 percent from British peers (3,154 total quotations were considered). The most frequently cited biblical book was Deuteronomy. Even when they quoted political thinkers, colonial authors used people like Algernon Sidney, who quoted the Bible frequently himself.[9]

Colonials noted especially those passages that condemned kings, and they observed the divine displeasure at Saul's election, which replaced the earlier "Hebraic Republic." Similarly they often quoted the law in Deuteronomy (Deut 17:14-20) that limited the powers of kings.[10] Thus, one may speak of the impact not only of biblical texts in general but also of antiroyal passages on the development of American democratic ideals. One notable example is the famous political essayist, Thomas Paine, whose pamphlet *Common Sense* sold 120,000 copies in a three-month period during 1776, which, considering the size of the American population at that time, makes this work proportionately the greatest bestseller in American history. Paine's work helped crystallize popular feeling for political independence from England. In this work Paine appealed to the story of how Gideon refused kingship, and he quoted much of 1 Samuel 8 wherein the prophet Samuel warned Israelites of the abuses of kingship and how their "idolatrous" quest for a king was the rejection of God.[11] "Paine reminded people of the words that had thundered down from colonial pulpits" for many years.[12]

The arguments of these authors dovetail excellently with the thesis of this book. Let us consider the message of the biblical text itself and see what raw biblical passages intelligentsia read two and three centuries ago, which led them to assail the institution of kingship and proclaim the equality of all people.

IV

Though kings in the ancient world and Israel provided a valuable role in the social structures of their age, they were critiqued by prophets and other biblical authors for their abuse of power and the oppression of the poor. Likewise, we today would praise our form of government and the value of many of our leaders. But we must not be blind to the fact that often leaders, who are complex human beings, as are we all, can do bad things to people. Power corrupts and absolute power corrupts absolutely. We must be alert to the abuse of power that can occur in our society. In this book I will attempt to show that the biblical text attacked and ridiculed kings and the institution of kingship. I will seek to unveil this critical stance in texts, such as Genesis 1–11, where commentators and average readers have not noticed it in the past. These biblical texts have influenced the development of our democratic thought, though most people are either unaware or do not wish to give sufficient credit to these texts. We should be thankful for our modern democratic institutions and grateful to the biblical text's contribution to their development. But this should not blind us to the fact that the human factor in human government endures throughout the ages and that even today the biblical text can be relevant in assailing the political abuse that still can occur. If we heed it, if we continue to proclaim the prophetic word, and if we seek to do something about political corruption in our own age, we may continue the living trajectory of that powerful message that was begun thousands of years ago.

Biblical scholars in the past generation are more inclined to look beneath the surface level of our biblical text, especially the narratives, and discern that the authors were uttering a word of contempt against their political leaders. Perhaps that is because those very first biblical authors may have cleverly masked subtle and critical observations in stories, which at first blush appear to praise those very leaders who originally heard and approved of the narratives that extolled their heroic virtues but were really designed to damn them. Perhaps in the later years of Jewish life in the first millennium B.C.E., the final editors of those stories looked back over sad and sorrowful centuries of past history, full of the incompetence and tyranny of kings, and they crafted accounts that

rendered a vision of the past with sometimes acerbic rhetorical condemnation and sometimes subtle ridicule. The books of 1 Kings and 2 Kings
have little patience with most of the kings of Israel and Judah from 930
to 586 B.C.E., and the historians who drew these traditions together
frequently passed judgment on them with heavy editorial comment. But
far more subtle are the stories about King David, the great founder, hero,
and archetype of the future messiah.

After a superficial reading of the text, which lends inspiration to Sunday school stories and grade-B movies in the portrayal of the great, heroic
David, one reads the text more closely and discerns the condemnation
of David's actions hidden beneath the surface of the narrative. Scholars
have recently unveiled the subtle judgment passed on David by the
biblical authors and later editors of the text. Most effective in this regard
is the work by Baruch Halpern, who views the accounts in 1 Samuel and
2 Samuel as attempts to explain away the bad things that happened when
David rose to power so as to legitimate his rule. Yet the text leaves us
enough clues to discover David's bloody and manipulative rise to power,
as witnessed in Halpern's subtitle of his book, *Messiah, Murderer, Traitor,
King*.[13] Of similar ilk is the volume by Stephen McKenzie, who evaluates
the development of the biblical literature through its stages of evolution.
He notes how critical evaluations are made of David in individual stories
even though the overall final composition is designed to legitimate the
Davidic dynasty as political apology.[14] Other authors approach the text
with an eye to the message produced by literary style of the narratives.
Stuart Lasine, in his own clever writing style, burrows into the stories
of David and other kings to discover irony and sarcasm designed to
condemn kings and the activities of those in power.[15] Robert Alter, a
master of evaluating biblical texts as great literature, sees beneath the
text and crafts an evaluation of David as the notorious king.[16] David's
successor and son, Solomon, has also received a revisionist evaluation.
Jung Ju Kang notes, through a close reading of the text, which considers
the rhetoric effect of the biblical passages, that the overall portrayal of
Solomon in these chapters has left a generally negative impression of
his reign, especially with his condemnation in 1 Kings 11, the concluding
chapter on his rule.[17] The text in chapter 11 judged, above all, Solomon's
actions in allowing foreign gods to come into the land through his wives.
J. G. McConville evaluates the narratives of Genesis through 2 Kings to
demonstrate how the Bible spoke of royal rule as an institution designed
to be subordinated to the rule of God, and therefore any tyrannical behavior by kings was condemned.[18] David Lamb studies the book of

Kings, and the traditions of King Jehu in particular, and concludes the biblical historian condemned hereditary kingship in favor of rule by prophets or temporary charismatic leaders.[19] Thus, there is a movement afoot in the past generation to discern the truly critical and deeper message of the text with regard to kings.

V

Many excellent scholarly works, too many to cite, have assessed the social-political evolution of kingship in Israel and Judah and how such an institution arose out of the highland pastoralist society of Israel during Iron Age I (1200–1050 B.C.E.). Among the many valuable insights these books have offered is the realization that our Bible was far less concerned with reporting the actual social, political, and economic details of state formation in Palestine than it was in providing a religious commentary on those events from the perspective of the later monotheistic authors. To be sure, helpful information is provided for us to reconstruct the political realities of that age. But we must not read the text literally without realizing that it is a subjective religious interpretation of an age that was already ancient by the time the biblical authors generated their history.

In their recall of the past, one of the central motifs for the theological historians was the importance of prophets or the spokespersons of Yahweh. Such people spoke an authoritative message and stood in judgment over the kings and leaders of the people because of their divine authorization. Needless to say, the actual Israelite and Judahite political leaders of that age did not believe that to be the case, but rather it was an interpretation of the past by biblical theologians who were trying to prepare a new future for their people. The critique of kings became very meaningful in the sixth-century B.C.E. Babylonian Exile as religious intelligentsia looked back and sought the reasons for the destruction of their people. The reason often given was the folly and oppression of kings. Had the kings listened to the prophetic representatives of Yahweh, the results of history could have been different; but the kings did not listen and exile resulted.

The Deuteronomistic Historians, authors of the books of Joshua, Judges, Samuel, and Kings, recalled the events of 1200 to 560 B.C.E. in an "after-the-fact" critique, not in an accurate portrayal of the actual political reality. Biblical texts might speak to us with a vision of nascent democracy, but there certainly was no sense of egalitarianism in the actual workings of those governments.[20] Rather, we see the idealistic vision found among the scribal intelligentsia who had the courage to speak of an alternative reality to the political system of their age. It is their vision that inspires us today, not the actual political reality of the ancient Israelites.[21]

In the past, several scholarly works described the biblical and pro-phetic critique of kings in Israel, tracing the history of that conflict in the life of the Israelites.[22] Often those works assumed that we could recon-struct the history of Israel from the Bible combined with contemporary sociological theory and that this resultant history testified to a revolu-tionary and egalitarian Israel existing in protest against kingship.[23] The model assumed an internal revolution of peasants against Canaanite kings and the establishment of an egalitarian society that was betrayed by the later Davidic and Solomonic monarchies but whose values were proclaimed anew by courageous prophets speaking out against the kings and their oppression.

This reconstruction of biblical history was a little too naive in the use of modern political categories and a little too optimistic about our ability to discover Israel's history. We are now more cautious about reconstruct-ing the social-political history from the biblical text, and we sense that much of the rhetoric of the biblical authors may be later in time (the exile) and a very idealistic and starker portrayal of Israel's history. For example, we now sense the conquest was a peaceful, internal process of with-drawal from the lowlands to the highlands by the peasants, not a peasant revolution. The kingdoms of David and Solomon were probably very small and not so well organized as we thought. True state formation did not arrive in Palestine until the middle of the eighth century B.C.E.[24] Nonetheless, the rhetoric of the biblical authors was valid and a real portrayal of the oppression that did occur under kings. Thus, those modern scholarly biblical theologies of the past generation still speak validly to us today about the message of justice in society and the need for modern social reform.

Biblical authors collected together prophetic oracles during the Baby-lonian Exile and beyond, and their selection of particular oracles reflected their later commentary of the preexilic world. Thus, we find especially critical memories of the royal and priestly preexilic leadership in pro-phetic books.

Likewise, in the epic literature of Genesis and Exodus we also discover a critique of the institution of kingship and an affirmation of the equality of all people. The criticism was conveyed in subtle and symbolic ways in narratives that were crafted in brilliant polyvalent fashion; that is, they communicated on many different levels of meaning in addition to their critique of kingship. Often we have observed the other meanings and slighted the anti-royal sentiment. We suspect that in their final form, as we have received them in the written canon, the biblical books also reflect the theological agenda of exilic and postexilic scribal authors.

The legal corpora, which we observe in the biblical text, are not really the direct laws by which everyday courts functioned. Rather, they were an ongoing and developing commentary on how justice should be administered in Israelite society by religious scribal intelligentsia.[25] The fact that those codes may not have been used does not diminish their rhetorical value as religiously inspired visions of a just and fair society functioning under the rule of a gracious and just deity.

Consideration of these narrative, prophetic, and legal texts should unveil for us that the biblical criticism of kingship goes well beyond anything in the ancient Near East. Many texts carry an implicit critique of the institution of kinship and its ideological underpinnings, while other texts recall an abrasive criticism of particular kings.

That these texts became part of the authoritative religious canon of Judaism and Christianity is significant, because they provided passages that average people could read. They planted the seeds of protest against authoritarian rule and played a role in the eventual demise of kings. After the printing press was invented by Gutenberg and great numbers of printed Bibles eventually were made available for average people, the revolutionary nature of these texts could influence the common folk. After the sixteenth century the fate of kingship would be sealed in Western Europe.

I suggest that as we observe the biblical critique of kings, we may notice that the biblical text speaks also of the fundamental equality of human beings. In articulating their beliefs, biblical authors provided for the Western tradition a religious authority for creating an egalitarian society.

2. Prophets

In the eighth century B.C.E. the classical prophets first appeared on the scene. They seem to be the first religious intelligentsia to criticize kings in any thoroughgoing fashion, if indeed our present reconstruction of how the biblical traditions evolved is correct. The prophetic spokespersons in the preexilic period may have preceded the formation of the written Pentateuchal narratives and the Deuteronomistic History (Joshua, Judges, Samuel, and Kings), both of which arose in the form in which we would recognize them during the sixth-century B.C.E. Babylonian Exile and in subsequent years. It appears to some commentators that the biblical authors who drew together the oral traditions and sometimes written fragments of literature to create the Pentateuch and the Historical Books may have been familiar with prophetic ideas. Thus, intellectually and theologically the classical prophets may have been foundational for the narrative traditions.

A century of tremendous economic and social change in both the northern state of Israel and the southern state of Judah witnessed the emergence of the great classical prophets. The middle of the eighth century B.C.E. saw economic development in Palestine caused by the emergence of the Assyrian Empire in Mesopotamia and the trade created by that empire throughout the Near East. International trade through the corridor of Palestine brought wealth to elite people in the larger cities of Samaria and Jerusalem, and these people used their wealth to create more wealth, as people in the modern age also do, often without regard for those weaker folk who might be hurt. Have we not seen in recent times how the greed of bankers, C.E.O.s, and mortgage lenders has destroyed our economic structures? Rich Israelites in Samaria and Judahites in Jerusalem in the eighth century B.C.E. participated in trade between the various sections of their own nations. Rich people bought the produce of peasants from some parts of the country and resold it in other parts of the country for high profit. Grain, cattle, olive oil, and wine moved throughout the country. Clever merchants and rich folk bought low and sold high, as the prophet Amos informs us, and they put poor people at a disadvantage, often using dishonest scales. They forced poor highland peasants into debt so that they could appropriate their farms under fictitious adoption guidelines, in order to maximize production on their newly acquired farms. They extended loans at high interest rates, and, when the poor peasant creditors defaulted, they were able to control them even more. Peasants were reduced to debt slavery and became the displaced poor in urban centers and subsequently the servants of the rich and powerful. Against these social abuses the classical prophets of the eighth century B.C.E. railed. From our perspective a new kind of prophet arose, whose style differed from previous prophets like Samuel, Nathan, Elijah, and Elisha (1050–800 B.C.E.), and their oral oracles would be written down and ultimately placed into our Old Testament. Amos, Hosea, Isaiah, and Micah spoke out on behalf of the poor who were being dispossessed in this time of economic change.

In addition, these prophets called for the exclusive worship of the national God, Yahweh, and obedience to the traditional customs and laws of the Yahwistic faith, which called for justice in society. Their cries for exclusive worship and obedience to Yahweh planted the seeds of monotheism, which would develop among the Israelite and the later Jewish populace as a whole in the sixth century B.C.E.

Some prophets spoke words of judgment against the people of Israel in the north (Amos and Hosea), while others addressed the people of Judah in the south (Isaiah and Micah). Though they condemned the two sins of oppressing the poor and worshiping other gods, they viewed these two sins as one. The worship of foreign gods permitted people to disregard the traditional values of highland Yahwistic culture with its inherent egalitarianism. There are numerous oracles in the prophetic corpus wherein prophets indicted kings for their sins. The kings, their relatives, and their friends in the cities of Samaria of Israel and Jerusalem of Judah were most responsible for taking advantage of poor highland peasants. Often kings were indicted along with priests and other government officials as the prophets bewailed the oppressive behavior of the "leaders." So there are frequent instances where kings were condemned without the specific reference to the word king.

II

The first classical prophet, Amos, is dated to the middle of the eighth century B.C.E. in the northern state of Israel. He was a thundering prophet of judgment who assaulted the rich and powerful for their oppression of the poor and their practices of seizing the land of poor highland peasant farmers. He attacked king Jeroboam II of Israel in acerbic fashion by declaring to Amaziah, priest of Bethel, that, "Jeroboam shall die by the sword, and Israel must go into exile away from his land" (Amos 7:11). To declare that the king should die, is a revolutionary act. That such a statement should be recorded in our biblical text by ancient authors is even more amazing. This is rhetoric one should expect in the modern age, not in the first millennium B.C.E. But Amos had a reason for his message: injustice originated, to a great extent, in the royal house in Samaria.

The rich and powerful people of Samaria benefited from royal policies that sponsored trade and land aggrandizement. Poor peasants were economically forced from their land by dubious practices of high interest rates and dishonest business practices to become debt slaves to the rich in the urban centers. With their new wealth, the affluent in Samaria bought luxury items such as ivory furniture. To such people Amos declared the following in Amos 3:15: "I will tear down the winter house as well as the summer house; and the houses of ivory shall perish, and the great houses shall come to an end." People of affluence owned two homes, one in the highlands for the summer, in order to escape the heat of the valleys, and one in the lowlands for the winter, in order to be warm. King Ahab of Israel, a century before Amos, owned a winter palace in Jezreel (1 Kgs 21:1) and a summer palace on Mount Samaria (1 Kgs 21:18). In these homes extravagant ivory furniture was purchased from foreign cities, like Damascus in Syria. Ahab also had such an "ivory palace" (1 Kgs 22:39). Excavations at Samaria by archaeologists have unearthed evidence of rich opulent homes with ivory inlays.[1]

To the wives of the rich Amos declared a ghoulish end in Amos 4:1-3,

> [1]Hear this word, you cows of Bashan who are on Mount Samaria, who oppress the poor, who crush the needy, who say to their husbands, "Bring something to drink!" [2]The Lord GOD has sworn by his holiness: The time is surely coming upon you, when they shall take you away with hooks, even the last of you with fishhooks. [3]Through breaches in the wall you shall leave, each one straight ahead; and you shall be flung out into Harmon, says the LORD.

Amos' anger was directed to the wives of rich men because their "afflu-ence was built on the suffering of the needy."[2] Bashan was an area of Israel in the northeast where fat cattle were bred to be butchered and eaten, and these cows were said to be fat and ferocious. So the rich women were compared to cows fattened for slaughter, but there was also a hint of meanness and ferocity. These upper-class women were envisioned as fat, opulent, self-indulgent, and arrogant.[3] The reference to their bodies being removed by hooks may have alluded to the Assyr-ian practice of removing dead bodies from a besieged city once it fell to their army. Bodies would be chopped up and body parts would be car-ried away in baskets. (At best this might have been simply a metaphor for exile, describing vividly how these arrogant women will be forced to walk hundreds of miles into exile in Assyria.) Amos implied that God would use the Assyrian army to punish the rich and powerful people in Samaria. Thirty years later the city of Samaria fell to Assyria after a three-year siege, and one can imagine how bloody that event was.

Amos repeated his dire threat of what would happen to the rich and powerful in Amos 6:4-7:

> [4]Alas for those who lie on beds of ivory, and lounge on their couches, and eat lambs from the flock, and calves from the stall; [5]who sing idle songs to the sound of the harp, and like David improvise on the instruments of music; [6]who drink wine from bowls, and anoint them-selves with the finest oils, but are not grieved over the ruin of Joseph! [7]Therefore they shall now be the first to go into exile, and the revelry of the loungers shall pass away.

The allusion to David may signal that the prophet spoke of the royal palace crowd. Certainly the life of luxury portrayed here makes us think of court dandies living with "expensive furniture, indolent ease, suc-culent food, the sound of music, and extravagant indulgence."[4] The word "lounge" means to hang loosely, like drapes or blankets. The Hebrew words evoke the imagery of these powerful lords "sprawled out in a stupor of satiation and drunkenness, no longer even able to control their own limbs."[5] But Amos said they would be exiled, a practice undertaken by Assyrian conquerors with their defeated victims—a custom designed to break the national spirit of a people.

Amos told the people of Samaria that a defeat at the hands of the mighty Assyrians was coming as punishment for how they oppressed the poor. They did not believe him. Then it came in 725–722 B.C.E. In a sense there was a connection between the degradation of the poor high-land peasants of Israel and the ultimate defeat by the Assyrian Empire. Oppression of the poor peasant classes of Israel, removal of highland farmers, and the concomitant seizure of their land alienated the common folk in Israel. Since the peasants would be drafted into the armies that defended Israel, one could imagine that the bulk of the soldiers in Israel's army fought only in halfhearted fashion and were defeated by the Assyrians in the field. Oppress the poor and you destroy the middle and lower classes, and the fabric of your society is weakened. We are doing this today, and if the backbone of the middle class is broken, then, indeed, our society will collapse too. If politicians favor the agenda of the rich, we will lose our middle class, as did ancient Israel. Increasingly in our country we discover that people lose their homes because they cannot pay mortgages they assumed, and someone made the commission for selling them this financial burden. In different ways, but with the same results, we seem to be breaking the back of our middle class. When this happens, eventually the entire social edifice of our society will collapse. But greedy people grasp with sticky hands all that they can hold without regard for the long-term destruction caused by their avarice.

III

Contemporary with Amos in the northern state of Israel was the prophet Hosea. While Amos was the social and economic critic of his society, Hosea directed most of his criticism toward religious issues in the northern state of Israel, such as veneration of the golden calf at Bethel. He did refer to the bad leadership of kings in several oracles. In Hos 5:1-2 we hear an indictment of both priests and the king:

> [1]Hear this, O priests! Give heed, O house of Israel! Listen, O house of the king! For the judgment pertains to you; for you have been a snare at Mizpah, and a net spread upon Tabor, [2]and a pit dug deep in Shittim; but I will punish all of them.

He did not give a particular reason for this word of judgment, but the dual condemnation of king and priests might indicate that Hosea excoriated them over the religious abuses in the land. It is possible that the three places listed all had shrines to Baal, which were sponsored by the political leaders.[6] The king especially would have had direct influence on how the cult was practiced, especially at Bethel, where the priest served at the beckon of the king. Both Amos and Hosea had bitter words for the religious worship undertaken at Bethel.

In Hos 5:10 a more concrete allusion appears. Hosea declared, "The princes of Judah have become like those who remove the landmark; on them I will pour out my wrath like water." The landmark was a boundary marker, usually a stone, placed between the properties of individual families. Someone who moved a boundary marker was a land thief, effectively stealing the property of his neighbor. Moving the boundary marking stone was considered a heinous crime. Princes and kings were called property thieves by Hosea, probably because they manipulated the economy to obtain the farmlands of bankrupted highland peasants. Moving a stone may seem at first appearance to be a small act, but its consequences for the victim can be great as the victimized family slowly loses farmland (Deut 19:14; 27:17; Prov 23:10; 22:28; Job 24:2). There are so many comparable customs in our society today wherein small actions put poor people at an economic disadvantage and thus sink them further into debt and despair.

In Hosea 7 several verses make rather vague references to kings. In v. 3 the prophet may have declared that dishonest people who engaged in evil acts made the king and officials glad.[7] Or it could be a reference to a palace revolution that overthrew one of Israel's rulers,[8] or perhaps a reference to the relatives and friends of the royal house who took advantage of the poor, given the social and legal environment created by the king. Often activities such as exorbitant interest rates, the prolonged retention of debt slaves, and legally sanctioned land seizures were made possible by royal policies and decisions. In vv. 5-7, however, the prophet described the gradual collapse of the state and the end of such political leaders. In v. 5 the officials of the king were overcome with wine, and in v. 7 it is said that the rulers were devoured and the kings have fallen. The references are unclear to us, but they certainly are words of judgment. Some commentators believe that this refers to a political assassination of one of the kings of Israel, or perhaps symbolically it refers to several assassinations.[9]

In Hos 8:4 a brief critique with profound implications was uttered, "They made kings, but not through me; they set up princes, but without my knowledge." This brief statement undercut the entire ancient Near Eastern understanding of the king as a representative or an incarnation of the deity. Hosea declared that the kings of Israel became kings by human design and not even with divine approval; certainly divine presence did not reside in them. Hosea might imply that kings were made without prophetic designation, which had occurred in the past.[10] In the same verse the prophet declared that idols were made by the people in the same way. This is a radical statement: that kings were a despicable human creation akin to crass idols.[11] Such a statement gutted the ideology undergirding the institution of kingship in the ancient world. In that same chapter the prophet said that people will "writhe under the burden of kings and princes" and this followed upon a statement that "they bargain with the nations." It seems that Hosea viewed these kings and princes as the foreigners, the Assyrians, who will eventually conquer Israel.

In Hos 10:3-4 the prophet attributed words to the people that certainly reflected his feelings about kings,

> [3]For now they will say: "We have no king, for we do not fear the LORD, and a king—what could he do for us?" [4]They utter mere words; with empty oaths they make covenants; so litigation springs up like poisonous weeds in the furrows of the field.

This particular translation attributes v. 4 to Hosea, so that the prophet described kings as speaking mere words and empty oaths. The powerlessness or shallowness of kings was emphasized here. Within a few verses the prophet declared in almost treasonous fashion, "Samaria's king shall perish like a chip on the face of the waters" (v. 7) and a little later we hear that "At dawn the king of Israel shall be utterly cut off" (v. 15), a clear anticipation of the destruction of the nation in 722 B.C.E. Such language would not be found elsewhere in the ancient world, for public spokespersons would not dare to speak of the impending death or destruction of the king.

Finally, a dramatic short oracle appears in Hos 13:9-11,

> [9]I will destroy you, O Israel; who can help you? Where now is your king, that he may save you? [10]Where in all your cities are your rulers, of whom you said, "Give me a king and rulers"? [11]I gave you a king in my anger, and I took him away in my wrath.

Sarcasm dripped from the prophet's lips as he spoke for God. God demanded to know from the people where was their king to save them from the great Assyrian threat. God said that the people demanded a king, perhaps an allusion to the story found in 1 Samuel 8, where the people requested a king from Samuel. Then God declared "I gave you kings, almost to punish you for the folly of that request, and then I took your kings away." What a bitter statement about the most revered being under the divine realm. Ancient kings declared that they were chosen by the gods, and kings in medieval and early modern European history made the same claim. Here God disavowed that entire ideology and said that people made kings against the divine will. The book of Hosea contained strong language against kings with a deep criticism of the entire institution, not just individual kings.[12] This critique resonated in later prophets and ultimately the Judeo-Christian tradition as a whole.

IV

A generation later, in the southern state of Judah, Isaiah made critical references to the folly of the king and his royal counselors. Isaiah was a prophet for a long period of time (c. 740–700 B.C.E.), and he appears to have functioned as a royal prophet serving in the Jerusalem courts of Kings Ahaz and Hezekiah. To Ahaz he was the unrelenting prophet of judgment, but to Hezekiah he spoke hope oracles, for the latter appeared to be more dedicated to the worship, perhaps exclusive worship, of Yahweh.

In oracles of judgment Isaiah could be acerbic in his criticism of kings. In Isa 1:10 he was particularly nasty when he addressed the rulers as though they were the "rulers of Sodom," an obvious allusion to corrupt leadership from the past. By this reference Isaiah probably meant that they were oppressive to the poor, for usually references to the sins of Sodom and Gomorrah focus on that sin rather than sexuality.

In Isa 1:23 the prophet declared, "Your princes are rebels and companions of thieves. Everyone loves a bribe and runs after gifts. They do not defend the orphan, and the widow's cause does not come before them." This passage probably alluded to what transpired in the courts. Kings often functioned as the highest court of appeal in the judicial system. The word for prince referred to rulers in general and included the king. Thus, Isaiah declared that even the king, as well as other rulers, would take a bribe to render a decision on behalf of the rich and powerful. Elsewhere in the ancient Near East kings and rulers proclaimed that they protected widows and orphans, especially in the law courts. It probably was not true, but kings in Mesopotamia and Egypt claimed that they did this. To explicitly declare that your rulers did not attend to the needs of widows and orphans in the courts was to directly use the stereotypical formula of that age in a way so as to condemn the ruler. In Isa 1:27 the prophet declared that God will give Jerusalem good rulers someday so that the city will be righteous and faithful. Even today as modern religious Jews and Christians enter the polling booth, we hope that the elected officials for whom we cast our ballots will be fair and honest and that they will not take bribes. But too often we too are disappointed by what our elected officials do (especially in Louisiana where I live). Here in Louisiana in the past ten years liberal Democrats were disappointed to discover one of their hopeful candidates for the future, Cleo Fields, walked out of a meeting with another politician with a large amount of cash. That other politician, a former governor, Edwin Edwards, later found himself in prison for other charges. Or again, a liberal Democrat who had served faithfully in congress for years, William Jefferson, had a shoebox full of bribe money hidden away in his freezer until the FBI found it. (Jokes about "cold cash" were common after that.) Conservative Republicans were chagrined to discover that one of their young, aggressive, and vocal politicians on the national scene, David Vitter, who had criticized Bill Clinton for his sexual indiscretions, maintained a Washington prostitute for a mistress at the same time that he spoke so boldly for family values. Disappointment strikes voters of both parties.

In Isa 2:7 the prophet made an oblique critique of kings when he declared that the land was filled with horses and chariots. Through vv. 6-8 the prophet stated that the land was full of various things because the people had forsaken God, and these things included diviners, soothsayers, silver, gold, treasures, horses, chariots, and idols, all of which were seen as bad. Obviously diviners and soothsayers were condemned because they engaged in divination. The silver, gold, and treasures are the wealth garnered by the rich and the powerful at the expense of the poor in any age. Idols of other gods or of Israel's god, Yahweh, obviously were condemned by the laws. The horses and the chariots, therefore, referred to the military equipment owned by the nation of Judah, not foreigners, and in particular, they were the weapons at the command of the king. The implication was that horses and chariots represented a royal capacity to make war, and they probably were purchased from other countries at a cost that inflicted an even greater economic burden on the poor. Judah did not raise horses, or craft chariots, since most probably they were purchased from Egypt with money that the king obtained by taxes. As is the case with any society, and especially our own, the ability to produce a sophisticated war technology entails spending valuable resources of a society, which eventually hurts the poor people more than anyone else. In our own country how much could have been spent on education, scientific research, medical research, social services, highways, and national infrastructure had we not put such a tremendous amount of money into advanced weapons systems over the past sixty years? In small African countries how much suffering occurs because the leaders have spent the national budget on First World weaponry, mostly from the United States?

In Isaiah 3 the prophet uttered a judgment oracle against the nation of Judah in which passing sarcastic allusions were made to kings and rulers whose very incompetence brought divine judgment on the people. In v. 4 the prophet declared that God will make "boys" and "babes" into the princes and rulers of the people. Great sarcasm is found in vv. 6-7:

> ⁶Someone will even seize a relative, a member of the clan, saying, "You have a cloak, you shall be our leader, and this heap of ruins shall be under your rule." ⁷But the other will cry out on that day, saying, "I will not be a healer; in my house there is neither bread nor cloak; you shall not make me leader of the people."

This is great humor. People sought to make someone king for the flimsiest of reasons over a nation that had completely fallen apart, and that person declined. Isaiah spoke abrasively of the political process in his own country. Do we not, even today, sometimes elect politicians for specious reasons, perhaps because they offer us promises, which we know they cannot or will not keep? But the promises appeal to our selfish instincts, and we vote for them. What do we then get? Bad leadership.

The prophet continued to excoriate the political leaders in the rest of Isaiah 3. In v. 12 the king and other political leaders were described as "children" who oppress the people and "women" who do the same. (We must remember that the biblical era was a patriarchal age, quite different from our own, wherein women were viewed as subordinate to men in the values of the popular culture, so that to call a leader a "woman" was to insult the person by implying that he was weak and ineffective. Old Testament laws frequently sought to elevate the rights of women, thus opposing the popular values of everyday society.) The prophet continued in v. 12 by saying that such leaders "mislead" and "confuse" the people.

Finally, the oracle in Isaiah 3 ended with a word of judgment against the leaders of Judah in vv. 14-15:

> [14]The LORD enters into judgment with the elders and princes of his people: It is you who have devoured the vineyard; the spoil of the poor is in your houses. [15]What do you mean by crushing my people, by grinding the face of the poor? says the Lord GOD of hosts.

With vivid clarity the prophet proclaimed that the powerful leaders have crushed the poor and ground down their faces. This is the ultimate message of the entire chapter.

The Immanuel Oracle found in Isa 7:13-25 was historically addressed to King Ahaz as a judgment oracle by the prophet, for it declared that the Assyrian army would devastate the countries all around Judah, thereby negatively affecting Judah also. Only later did the Immanuel motif evolve into an image of hope. In Isa 7:13 Isaiah told Ahaz that as king he "wearies" both humans and God. Such language from a court prophet may reflect the license that a court prophet could have had when addressing the king, but its preservation for all time in our written text provides a constant reminder that the prophet of God could stand in judgment over the king. Truly the king's power was limited according to the prophetic witness.

Powerful images of hope were connected to an ideal figure who would come someday according to the oracles of Isaiah. Isa 9:6-7 declared that a child will be born who shall be called "Wonderful Counselor, Mighty God, Everlasting Father, Prince of Peace," and we suspect that Isaiah was talking about a future ideal king. Perhaps he spoke this oracle early in the reign of king Hezekiah of Judah, hoping that Hezekiah would be that ideal king. But eventually after both Hezekiah and Isaiah died, this oracle would be remembered and envisioned as a description of the ideal king to come, and ultimately Christians would connect the vision of hope with Jesus. Critical scholars suggest that these words may have been taken from Egyptian coronation language rituals, and the court in Judah may have taken the language over to apply to Judahite kings at their coronation.[13] If so, it is royal language. But it also carried a nuance of judgment against kings in general. For so many, if not all, kings fell short of this image that one could almost construe this rhetoric as a criticism of any reigning king, for it declared that someday a truly righteous king would come. Isa 11:1-5 carried this imagery even further. The prophet declared that a "shoot shall come out from the stump of Jesse" (v. 1) who was the father of David, thus making this an allusion to the royal line of kings in Judah. The "spirit of the Lord" will give him wisdom, understanding, counsel, might, knowledge, and the fear of the

Lord (v. 2). This person shall judge the poor with righteousness and "decide with equity for the meek of the earth" (v. 4). This just king obviously would put to shame all the kings who have ruled Judah and Israel otherwise, not to mention the kings of the nations. To speak of such an ideal king in this fashion actually condemned real kings for their shortcomings. Prior to the end of time, no human king will meet this high level of expectation, and "the ideal king of Isa 11:1-5 will always be a promised future ruler."[14]

V

Micah was a prophet, contemporary with Isaiah, who may have spoken oracles around 710–700 B.C.E., when the country of Judah was extensively damaged by war with Assyria. We know little of him. His use of legal language tempts scholars to suggest he was a rural elder who functioned as a judge. Chapters 1–3, 6 contain oracles of judgment and in the opinion of most scholars they come from Micah. Chapters 4–5, 7 contain oracles of hope and may have originated with Micah or might come from a prophet two centuries later. A word of judgment found in Mic 3:1 declared, "Listen, you heads of Jacob and rulers of the house of Israel! Should you not know justice?" Of course, the implication was that they did not. "The leaders of Israel presided over an administration of injustice in the courts" where "they flay and devour the plaintiffs instead of hearing their plea."[15] Later in that same chapter the prophet proclaimed,

> 9Hear this, you rulers of the house of Jacob and chiefs of the house of Israel, who abhor justice and pervert all equity, 10who build Zion with blood and Jerusalem with wrong! 11Its rulers give judgment for a bribe, its priests teach for a price, its prophets give oracles for money; yet they lean upon the Lord and say, "Surely the Lord is with us! No harm shall come upon us."

Notice the last verse. Corrupt rulers oppressed the poor, took bribes, and despised justice, then proclaimed that the Lord was on their side. "With God on our side," they declared they would be safe. One is painfully reminded of how often we Americans say or assume that God is on our side also. Do our leaders take advantage of the poor, take bribes, and twist the legal system of our land? Somehow the words of the prophet seem painfully timeless! After this last refrain Micah proclaimed that "Zion shall be plowed as a field; Jerusalem shall become a heap of ruins" (Mic 3:12). Is this a word of warning we should heed today?

If Mic 5:2-5 came from the eighth-century B.C.E. prophet Micah and not a nameless prophet from a later age, then it insulted existing kings by portraying the image of an ideal ruler who would arise someday, who would be so unlike the rulers on the throne.[16] This ruler will come from Bethlehem, as did David, and he will "feed his flock in the strength of the Lord" and the people "shall live secure," for he shall "be the one of peace." We know not of whom the prophet spoke. Perhaps he hoped that King Hezekiah of Judah would be an ideal king, or perhaps the prophet simply envisioned that someday an ideal king would arise. This is the case if the oracle comes from the sixth century B.C.E. when the Jews no longer had kings. Ultimately, of course, Christians saw the oracle fulfilled ultimately in Jesus, whose very identity as king condemned all who call themselves king in this world.

3. Jeremiah and Ezekiel

I

The Deuteronomic Reform movement was inspired by the earlier eighth-century B.C.E. prophets and sought to create a just society, focus exclusive religious devotion on Yahweh, and provide guidelines by which to limit the power of kings. When King Josiah died in 609 B.C.E., the movement was discredited in the minds of many in Judah, and people, including the kings, began to return to the old social and religious patterns of behavior. We know from the later prophets and archaeology that people were staunchly polytheistic in this era, and the critical words of the prophets testify to the social injustice. Though the Deuteronomic Reform movement failed, the destruction of the nation in 586 B.C.E. caused some religious intelligentsia to hearken back to the ideals of this movement. People in exile listened to that message, elevated this literature, and sought to rebuild the life and religious values of Jews in exile. Ultimately this renewed commitment created Second Temple period Judaism and the beginnings of the Old Testament.

Prophetic spokespersons, who defended the values of monotheistic faith and social justice, may have been responsible, in part, for the emergence of Judaism out of the ashes of its 586 B.C.E. destruction. These prophets also continued the criticism of kings. They saw that the collapse of the nation was due to the political and religious policies of their political leaders. Their words are worth heeding yet today.

II

Before the destruction of Jerusalem and the temple in 586 B.C.E., Jeremiah defended the values of the Deuteronomic Reform movement after

Josiah's death. The burden of his prophetic ministry was great, for he proclaimed a message that was discredited in the minds of many. He proclaimed his message to avert national disaster by calling the people of Judah to repent of their sins and turn to the exclusive worship of God, and he was abrasive in his rebuke of contemporary kings. References to the sinful actions of kings may be found throughout the book of Jeremiah, but an especially long diatribe against Judah's kings is located in Jeremiah 21–22. In Jer 21:1–22:30 we find oracles against the various kings of Judah in those last years of national existence: Zedekiah, Jer 21:1–22:10; Jehoahaz, Jer 22:10-12; Jehoiakim, Jer 22:13-19; and Jehoiachin, Jer 22:20-30 (though that is not their chronological order). It has been observed that the collection of all these antiroyal oracles in one place has a cumulative effect of destroying the sacredness of the institution of kingship.[1]

In Jer 21:1-10 the prophet proclaimed that King Zedekiah (the last of Judah's kings) would be taken into exile in Babylon. A dramatic imperative was given to Zedekiah in Jer 21:12:

> O house of David! Thus says the LORD: Execute justice in the morning, and deliver from the hand of the oppressor anyone who has been robbed, or else my wrath will go forth like fire, and burn, with no one to quench it, because of your evil doings.

Kings throughout the ancient world were regarded as the people most responsible for ensuring that there was justice in the court systems.

An unidentified king was condemned in Jer 22:6-7:

> [6]You are like Gilead to me, like the summit of Lebanon; but I swear that I will make you a desert, an uninhabited city. [7]I will prepare destroyers against you, all with their weapons; they shall cut down your choicest cedars and cast them into the fire.

Strong language here assaulted the king, for Jeremiah compared the king to a ravaged city, obviously an allusion to what could happen to the city of Jerusalem.

A short oracle in Jer 22:10-12 alluded to Shallum or Jehoahaz, who was quickly removed from the throne by the invading Egyptians after three months of rule:

> [10]Do not weep for him who dead, nor bemoan him; weep rather for him who goes away, for he shall return no more to see his native land. [11]For thus says the LORD concerning Shallum son of King Josiah

of Judah, who succeeded his father Josiah, and who went away from this place: He shall return here no more, ¹²but in the place where they have carried him captive he shall die, and he shall never see this land again.

A judgment oracle against Jehoiachin (Coniah) in Jer 22:24-30 stated that Yahweh would tear the king off of his divine finger:

> ²⁴As I live, says the LORD, even if King Coniah son of Jehoiakim of Judah were the signet ring on my right hand, even from there I would tear you off ²⁵and give you into the hands of those who seek your life, into the hands of those of whom you are afraid, even into the hands of King Nebuchadrezzar of Babylon and into the hands of the Chaldeans. ²⁶I will hurl you and the mother who bore you into another country, where you were not born, and there you shall die. ²⁷But they shall not return to the land to which they long to return.
> ²⁸Is this man Coniah a despised broken pot, a vessel no one wants? Why are he and his offspring hurled out and cast away in a land that they do not know? ²⁹O land, land, land, hear the word of the LORD! ³⁰Thus says the LORD: Record this man as childless, a man who shall not succeed in his days; for none of his offspring shall succeed in sitting on the throne of David, and ruling again in Judah.

Jehoiachin was exiled in 597 B.C.E. after a very brief reign, for his predecessor, Jehoiakim, had died shortly before the Chaldean Babylonians arrived to besiege Jerusalem and take captives. Jehoiachin inherited the political disaster created by Jehoiakim. But Jeremiah had no respect for him either. This is incredibly strong language, almost treasonous in its tone. He declared that the king would go into exile and would have no offspring to succeed him, a horrible thought for any king. But the most abrasive imagery was used by Jeremiah against King Jehoiakim, the ruler prior to Jehoiachin. In Jer 22:13-17 Jehoiakim's greed was attacked as he was contrasted to his righteous father, Josiah, who died in 609 B.C.E.:

> ¹³Woe to him who builds his house by unrighteousness, and his upper rooms by injustice; who makes his neighbors work for nothing, and does not give them their wages; ¹⁴who says, "I will build myself a spacious house with large upper rooms," and who cuts out windows for it, paneling it with cedar, and painting it with vermilion. ¹⁵Are you a king because you compete in cedar? Did not your father eat and drink and do justice and righteousness? Then it was well with him. ¹⁶He judged the cause of the poor and needy; then it

was well. Is not this to know me? says the LORD. [17]But your eyes and heart are only on your dishonest gain, for shedding innocent blood, and for practicing oppression and violence.

For these reasons Jeremiah concluded that Jehoiakim deserved the burial of an ass (Jer 22:18-19), a most disgraceful image:

> [18]Therefore thus says the LORD concerning King Jehoiakim son of Josiah of Judah: They shall not lament for him, saying, "Alas, my brother!" or "Alas, sister!" They shall not lament for him, saying, "Alas, lord!" or "Alas, his majesty!" [19]With the burial of a donkey he shall be buried—dragged off and thrown out beyond the gates of Jerusalem.

How incredible that the prophet could declare of his king that he deserved nothing better than to be treated like an ass. This particular bit of invective came after Jeremiah described the righteous behavior of Josiah, the father of Jehoiakim, in judging the cause of the poor and needy (Jer 22:15-16). For over two thousand years Jews and Christians have heard Jeremiah declare that a king deserved the burial of an ass because of his unjust treatment of poor people. Is this not a text that can eventually inspire revolution against kings and the creation of a democratic society? Like a time bomb it has been sitting in the Bible waiting to make its influence felt in the revolutionary and evolutionary advance of human religious and social values.

Jeremiah 23 began a new collection of oracles to be distinguished from the judgment upon the various kings in Jeremiah 21–22, but it is a fitting sequel. It began with a condemnation of the shepherds or kings who were declared responsible for the exile of the Jews. We read in Jer 23:1-4:

> [1]Woe to the shepherds who destroy and scatter the sheep of my pasture! says the LORD. [2]Therefore thus says the LORD, the God of Israel, concerning the shepherds who shepherd my people: It is you who have scattered my flock, and have driven them away, and you have not attended to them. So I will attend to you for your evil doings, says the LORD. [3]Then I myself will gather the remnant of my flock out of all the lands where I have driven them, and I will bring them back to their fold, and they shall be fruitful and multiply. [4]I will raise up shepherds over them who will shepherd them, and they shall not fear any longer, or be dismayed, nor shall any be missing, says the LORD.

This oracle was a transition, summarizing the evil done by the old kings, but offering hope of future kings who will be good. Of course, such kings never came to rule Judah. But the image of the future righteous king, this powerful image of hope, was yet again another condemnation of real kings in real life, most of whom could never and would never act with such nobility. So the prophet spoke a word of hope in Jer 23:5-6:

> ⁵The days are surely coming, says the Lord, when I will raise up for David a righteous Branch, and he shall reign as king and deal wisely, and shall execute justice and righteousness in the land. ⁶In his days Judah will be saved and Israel will live in safety. And this is the name by which he will be called: "The Lord is our righteousness." [This oracle is repeated with only minor differences in Jer 33:14-16.]

Elsewhere in the book of Jeremiah there were other passing critical allusions to kings. In Jer 2:26-27 the prophet stated,

> ²⁶As a thief is shamed when caught, so the house of Israel shall be shamed—they, their kings, their officials, their priests, and their prophets, ²⁷who say to a tree, "You are my father," and to a stone, "You gave me birth." For they have turned their backs to me, and not their faces. But in the time of their trouble they say, "Come and save us!"

Leaders, including kings, were compared to a thief. Sarcastically they were said to worship trees and stones. The trees probably were a symbol for the fertility goddess Asherah, and devotion to her was still very popular in Jeremiah's age. Kings tried to make everyone happy by worshiping all the gods of their people, just as candidates make many promises to various constituencies today, which contradict each other and cannot be kept. Every candidate promises to cut taxes and then promises new programs by which to help society. Shame on the voters who believe them! Jeremiah berated the kings for their casual worship of various gods and the objects used to represent those gods. Of course, they would turn to Yahweh, the national deity, in time of trouble, just like people might do today. Jeremiah leaves us with the impression that these royal personages were stupid.

In Jer 24:9-10 Jeremiah spoke of Zedekiah, the last king of Judah before the fall, and again made abrasive statements about Zedekiah's future, as well as that of his officials:

> ⁹I will make them a horror, an evil thing, to all the kingdoms of the earth—a disgrace, a byword, a taunt, and a curse in all the places where I shall drive them. ¹⁰And I will send sword, famine, and pestilence upon them, until they are utterly destroyed from the land that I gave to them and their ancestors.

In several oracles Jeremiah condemned the bad shepherds. Usually the image of a shepherd was a metaphor throughout the ancient Near East for the king, so that these oracles contained oblique references to the abusive behavior of kings. In Jer 12:10-11 Jeremiah spoke of how the shepherds destroyed God's vineyard. In Jer 25:34-38 the prophet proclaimed that the day of destruction for the shepherds had come. They should "roll in ashes" (v. 34) for their slaughter would come and there would be "no escape" (v. 35). The last king of Judah, Zedekiah, was captured after fleeing the city of Jerusalem, his sons were killed before his eyes, and then he was blinded and led away in chains to Babylon (Jer 39:1-8). The threatening words of the prophet came true.

In Jer 34:2-3 Jeremiah spoke to Zedekiah of his eventual fate:

> ²Thus says the LORD: I am going to give this city into the hand of the king of Babylon, and he shall burn it with fire. ³And you yourself shall not escape from his hand, but shall surely be captured and handed over to him; you shall see the king of Babylon eye to eye and speak with him face to face; and you shall go to Babylon.

Indeed, as noted previously, this describes well what actually transpired for the last king of Judah. To recall that such things happened to the king was not only humiliating for the king but was also a humiliating memory for the institution of kingship.[2]

Finally, a somewhat entertaining story was told about Jeremiah and King Jehoiakim in Jeremiah 36. It was told with "such a wealth of circumstantial detail" that commentators suggest this was an eyewitness report.[3] Jeremiah was directed by God to make a scroll containing his judgment oracles, and this was read before the king (vv. 2-3). Jeremiah's scribe, Baruch, wrote down the oracles and took the scroll to the king (vv. 4-7). After Baruch publicly read the scroll (vv. 9-10), he was asked to reread it to the royal officials (vv. 11-19). When the king found out about the scroll, he seized it, cut it into shreds, and burned each piece in the fire of his brazier (vv. 20-26) in an obvious attempt to negate the "magical power" of the scroll. The king viewed the scroll as having magical power because the oral message of the prophet's oracles was now converted into written form, giving the oracles more power. So the king countered this power of the written word by destroying it. Jeremiah heard of this and simply had Baruch write another scroll (vv. 27-28, 32). He then stated of the king that, "He shall have no one to sit upon the throne of David, and his dead body shall be cast out to the heat by day and the frost by night" (v. 30). This was the same king of whom Jeremiah said that he deserved the burial of an ass. In general, the story tells us of a classic confrontation between the prophet and the king. But it also shows us a king who regarded the oracles of the prophet as being like curses, which had to be countered by some dramatic magical act of burning. Obviously, the prophet Jeremiah found this to be foolish and he simply recreated the scroll. The whole story then cast the king in a very negative light as a superstitious fool.

III

Ezekiel was active as a prophet to exiles in Babylon from about 593 to 571 B.C.E. He was among the Jews taken to Babylon in the first exile of 597 B.C.E., so he thus spoke of the impending destruction of Jerusalem and the exile of all Jews in 586 B.C.E., even though he was already in exile. Prior to Jerusalem's destruction he was a prophet of doom; after that time he became a prophet of hope.

In many ways Ezekiel's message paralleled that of his contemporary, Jeremiah. For example, Ezekiel's judgment on the shepherds (the kings of Israel and Judah) in Ezek 34:2-10 furthered the rhetorical imagery of Jeremiah about the shepherds:

> ²Ah, you shepherds of Israel who have been feeding yourselves! Should not shepherds feed the sheep? ³You eat the fat, you clothe yourselves with the wool, you slaughter the fatlings; but you do not feed the sheep. ⁴You have not strengthened the weak, you have not healed the sick, you have not bound up the injured, you have not brought back the strayed, you have not sought the lost, but with force and harshness you have ruled them. ⁵So they were scattered, because there was no shepherd; and scattered, they became food for all the wild animals. ⁶My sheep were scattered, they wandered over all the mountains and on every high hill; my sheep were scattered over all the face of the earth, with no one to search or seek for them.

> [7]Therefore, you shepherds, hear the word of the LORD: [8]As I live, says the Lord GOD, because my sheep have become a prey, and my sheep have become food for all the wild animals, since there was no shepherd; and because my shepherds have not searched for my sheep, but the shepherds have fed themselves, and have not fed my sheep; [9]therefore, you shepherds, hear the word of the LORD: [10]Thus says the Lord GOD, I am against the shepherds; and I will demand my sheep at their hand, and put a stop to their feeding the sheep; no longer shall the shepherds feed themselves. I will rescue my sheep from their mouths, so that they may not be food for them.

One can readily observe the great similarities with Jeremiah's oracles on shepherds. Ezekiel functioned in Mesopotamia where the image of the shepherd was a common metaphor used by kings to describe their relationship to their people (as also in Palestine).[4] Ezekiel metaphored the shepherds or kings as eating their sheep, the people, rather than protecting them (v. 3), an obvious allusion to how the kings took advantage of the people. This misrule by the kings led to the scattering or exile of the sheep, or the Jews, all over the face of the earth (vv. 5-6). God opposed these evil shepherds (v. 10) and promised to deliver the people from the hands of their kings. A much later generation obviously could be inspired by this passage to overthrow the institution of kingship.

As Jeremiah spoke disparagingly of king Zedekiah and his ultimate doom, so also Ezekiel referred to this same king in Ezek 12:10-14[5]:

> [10]Say to them, "Thus says the Lord GOD: This oracle concerns the prince in Jerusalem and all the house of Israel in it." [11]Say, "I am a sign for you: as I have done, so shall it be done to them; they shall go into exile, into captivity." [12]And the prince who is among them shall lift his baggage on his shoulder in the dark, and shall go out; he shall dig through the wall and carry it through; he shall cover his face, so that he may not see the land with his eyes. [13]I will spread my net over him, and he shall be caught in my snare; and I will bring him to Babylon, the land of the Chaldeans, yet he shall not see it; and he shall die there. [14]I will scatter to every wind all who are around him, his helpers and all his troops; and I will unsheathe the sword behind them.

Ezekiel's angry vision, like that of Jeremiah's, indeed came true.

Ezekiel's highly symbolic oracle against the king of Tyre (Ezek 28:1-19) should be interpreted as a general criticism of kings, for there is nothing for us to link it to a specific king or Tyre or any country, but rather it was a description of the ancient Near Eastern ideological view of kings.[6] The prophet's attack on the Phoenician king of Tyre was crafted in such a way as to compare him to the first man, Adam, in Genesis 2–3. Ezekiel's knowledge of the account of the first man differed from our version of Genesis 2–3 in several interesting ways: though the sin was pride and the desire to be like God, there was no tree or fruit, no woman, no snake, and the garden was on a mountain. We sometimes suspect that Ezekiel's version may be an older version from which Genesis 2–3 was derived. But the persona was a king, and the judgment oracle may have spoken about the nature of kings in general.

The oracle about the king of Tyre described him as having a proud heart and claiming to be a god (v. 2), which is what many kings in the ancient Near East claimed to be—a divine being sent to live among and rule mortals. This ancient ideology created an "exaltation of human caprice into a divine right" and led to "claims to superhuman wisdom" and the right to attain power and wealth.[7] Ezekiel admitted that the king was wise, wealthy, and successful in trade (vv. 3-5). But the king of Tyre would face a military attack (v.7), and he would be killed and thrown into the "Pit," or the underworld (vv. 8-10). Ezekiel further described the king as perfect and blameless, living in Eden among precious stones (like Revelation 21), and guarded by a cherubim (vv. 11-15), reminding us again of Genesis 2–3. But this rich and powerful being was guilty of violence, pride, and sin, and thus deserved to die and to be burned to ashes (vv.16-19). The king of Tyre was a paradigm for all kings.

In Ezekiel 31–32 the prophet attacked Pharaoh of Egypt in a similar tirade. Pharaohs in Egypt claimed to be the living incarnation of the god Horus in this life, and once deceased they became the god Osiris in the underworld. Hence, the image of a king who claimed divine status once more was the target of the prophet's rhetorical wrath. Pharaoh was compared to a proud cedar of Lebanon, a tree that will be destroyed and sent down into the "Pit" (Ezek 32:2-17). This tree was described by the prophet in such a way as to imply that it is the great "world tree" in the center of the cosmos, in the garden of the gods, which sends its roots down into the cosmic deeps and has the power of divine life, an image found in the folklore of Mesopotamians (the Kishkanu tree in Eridu and the sacred tree in the Irra Epic), Teutons (ash-tree in Edda), Indians (Buddha's Bo Tree), and Chinese.[8] (Obviously this symbolic tree inspired the narrative in Genesis 2–3 about the "Tree of Life" and the "Tree of Knowledge." In Ezek 31:18 this tree was said to be in Eden.) Ancient Near Easterners associated their rulers with such a mythical "tree of life." But the prophet stated that the tree would be destroyed. In Ezek 31:18, Pharaoh was told that he will be cut down with this tree of Eden and sent to the underworld. In Ezekiel 32 the prophet again addressed Pharaoh, comparing him to a dragon who will be dragged up forth, thrown on the ground, killed, cut up, and devoured by the animals (vv. 2-6), then subsequently paraded captive before the nations (vv. 9-10) after defeat by the king of Babylon (vv. 11-16). The prophet evoked literary imagery from the Mesopotamian creation myth, the *Enuma Elish*, which told how Marduk killed female Tiamat, who was the great chaotic waters and was symbolized by a great seven-headed dragon, and how Marduk then cut up her body to make the Mesopotamian river valley.[9]

When we consider these two oracles together, the tirades against the king of Tyre and Pharaoh of Egypt, we see the prophet assaulting some of the common ancient assumptions about the nature of kingship: that kings are divine; wielders of great power; wise; patrons of building projects, trade, and the arts because of their exalted status. Ezekiel brought them back down to earth, or, more appropriately, he brought them down into the "Pit," death, and the underworld. I believe that we should more readily speak of Ezekiel's assault upon kingship in general in these passages, and not simply describe them as attacks upon Tyre and Egypt.

At this point it is worth turning to Isaiah 14, for it is an oracle that has some connection to Ezekiel 28 in the minds of many commentators. It spoke of the fall of the king of Babylon in symbolic and mythic terms, comparable to how Ezekiel described the fall of the king of Tyre and Pharaoh. The oracle in Isa 14:3-21 is often dated by commentators to the time of the Babylonian Exile of the Jews, the age in which Ezekiel lived. Some attribute it to the prophet who proclaimed the oracles in Isaiah 40–55, whom we call Second Isaiah. The oracle referred to images such as the cedars of Lebanon who exulted over the king of Babylon (v. 8) and the "Pit" into which the king of Babylon came (vv. 9-16), themes we observed in Ezekiel's oracles. The king of Babylon was cast into the pit of Sheol (the underworld), just as the man of Tyre was thrown off the mountain into the pit of Sheol. There all the dead leaders of the past mocked the king because his pomp was gone and he became as weak as they were (vv. 9-11). The king of Babylon was compared to the rising and setting "Day Star," or the planet Venus, who was the symbol for Ishtar, goddess of Babylon. As Venus went below the horizon at certain times during the year, or when it was outshone by the sun,[10] so the king went down to Sheol. Like the king of Tyre, the king of Babylon was described as being on a sacred mountain (vv. 13-14), from which he descended into Sheol. People then reflected over the humiliation of his descent and death (vv. 15-21). With this oracle, I believe, we have again a prophetic critique not only of the specific king of Babylon, but of kings in general. Prophets were not content simply to insult the kings of Israel and Judah, they attacked all the kings of the ancient world.

IV

Though there obviously are passages in the prophetic corpus that speak of good kings, and especially an ideal king who will come in the future (messiah), I wish to stress the presence of these negative comments against kings. They were uttered by prophets who believed that kings failed in their responsibility to serve people as the true representatives of God. By itself this observation would not make the prophets into antimonarchical revolutionaries. But the prophetic oracles combined with the Deuteronomistic narratives give us the image of a prophet proclaiming a word from God that is to be regarded as superior to the authority of the king. This theological image cut at the heart of royal ideology in the ancient world. The prophets attacked the very assumptions in which kingship was rooted. The biblical worldview separated the king from the divine so that the king was not God. Not only was God higher than the king, so also was the prophetic word, spoken by another human being, a higher authority. This higher authority claimed its origin in the mind of God, whence came the prophetic oracles, but the social-historical reality was that human beings, or prophets, spoke these words. Once these prophetic oracles and stories were proclaimed, it would only be a matter of time before people figured out the implications and deduced that perhaps they might be well to do away with kings completely. Of course, the prophets themselves would not have considered the elimination of kingship. The first millennium B.C.E. was not ready for that social-political advance. But their message would pave the way for such ideas someday.

Prophets elsewhere in the ancient world, such as those at the ancient Mesopotamian city of Mari in the middle of the second millennium B.C.E., gave oracles that chided the king for his failure to attend to the shrine of the deity in some particular city or the failure to renovate a temple. But Israelite prophets were more radical in their critique, attacking the very assumptions of divine kingship and the concomitant right to rule people with absolute authority. Both the preexilic prophets who spoke these words and the exilic and postexilic scribes who recorded them in our prophetic works exhibit a deep intellectual assumption concerning the finitude of the institution of kingship, which appears not to be shared by any of their contemporaries in the ancient Near East and can only be paralleled by similar rhetoric out of later classical Greece. Some commentators have found this foundational attack upon the institution of kingship to be one of the most signal contributions of the Hebrew Bible and the inspiration for the later emergence of democratic thought.[11]

Concomitant with the prophetic critique of kings was another belief not only of the prophets but of the Yahwistic movement as a whole—that all people are equal before God. Combined with the prophetic critique of kingship and kings, this foundational religious concept found in both Judaism and Christianity eventually spelled the death knell for kings.

4. Laws

Law codes in the ancient Near East were given to society from the gods through the mediation of kings. This, at least, was the fiction that kings maintained, for it strengthened their political power over their societies. When one reflects upon the lawgiving process in Israel, it is most apparent that Moses performed the role of mediator, for he received the laws from God up on Sinai and then brought them down to the people. Moses was no king; he usurped the role of king, most evidently in his function of wrenching slaves away from the control of a king, Pharaoh. Moses is an antiking, the liberator of slaves. His birth narrative, which we shall discuss in a later chapter, brings his role as an antiking into sharp focus. He became a prince in Egypt only after he was born a slave. When he went to the wilderness, therein was the presence of God to be found, not in the palaces or the temples of the urban centers. Moses was commissioned by God to return to Egypt, where he then liberated the slaves from the king—Pharaoh—and took them to the wilderness. In the wilderness at the mountain, Moses performed the supposed role of a king by giving the escaped slaves laws that provided for them a sense of identity. But Moses was a prophet, not a king. Laws came to the people through Moses, and in a deeper sense the laws really came directly from God to the people. Furthermore, the laws seldom mentioned a king, which was even a further slight to the institution of royalty.

It is obvious to us that the kings of Israel and Judah promulgated laws, but the biblical authors have suppressed that memory by attributing the generation of all the laws to Moses in an age before the emergence of kings in Israel.[1] This implies that one of the most important royal functions in the ancient world was not performed by Israel's kings.

In the ancient world laws and law codes often were promulgated in the context of covenantal relationship between the god(s) and the king, who represented the people before the gods and in turn was a god to the people. But in Israel the covenant was established without a king, symbolically made in the wilderness, at the foot of a mountain, between God and recently escaped slaves. This was a revolutionary concept, that God could make a legal relationship or covenant directly with the people. This image of the covenant made between God and people inspired the early Pilgrim and Puritan settlers in New England, as well as subsequent Americans. In those early years the American colonists frequently spoke in covenantal language in political contexts.

Allow people who are ruled by kings to read these passages long enough, and they will decide that they no longer need kings. Once the Bible became available in English translation, especially after the 1611 King James Bible, people began to make that assumption. We recall especially how the first Pilgrim settlers in the new world spoke of their covenant, for example, with the creation of the Mayflower Compact. Covenant language, taken from the Bible, was language that dispensed with kings. Those settlers, consciously or unconsciously, were on their way to dispensing with their kings.

In biblical law texts, the law was given to people without need for an earthly king. Whether this language arose early in Israel's history or whether it came later from the circles of Deuteronomistic Historians in the late seventh century B.C.E., it still originated in the first millennium B.C.E., and it was revolutionary for its age. What was most revolutionary was not necessarily what was said but rather what was not said, what was missing—the king. We do not need to see language in the laws about the wickedness of kings; the mere fact that they were missing is our message.[2]

There was one passage in the legal tradition that spoke of kings. This most important text concerning the institution of kingship was in the Deuteronomic Reform Law Code. The Deuteronomic Code contained laws that may have emerged as early as the eighth century B.C.E. in oral form, but in their present written form the Code most likely emerged in the late seventh-century B.C.E. reform movement of Josiah of Judah (with some exilic additions from the sixth century B.C.E.). In Deut 17:14-20 we find legislation designed to limit the power of the king, a concept that violently goes against the prevailing ideologies throughout the ancient Near East. Although the issues addressed by this law were not broad in scope, nor did they provide rights for the common people that we in the modern era affirm; nonetheless, the law limited the power of kings in regard to matters of royal self-glorification. That fact that such a law could even exist in the ancient world is amazing.[3] We have to wait until the thirteenth-century C.E. Magna Charta (or Magna Carta) in England to find a comparable notion that royal power should be limited. We fail to appreciate how revolutionary this text in Deuteronomy was for its age because we bask in the sunshine of constitutional democratic liberty in our own era. Yet in some way this biblical text laid the foundation for our modern rights. The text reads as follows,

> [14]When you have come into the land that the LORD your God is giving you, and have taken possession of it and settled in it, and you say, "I will set a king over me, like all the nations that are around me," [15]you may indeed set over you a king whom the LORD your God will choose. One of your own community you may set as king over you; you are not permitted to put a foreigner over you, who is not of your own community. [16]Even so, he must not acquire many horses for himself, or return the people to Egypt in order to acquire more horses, since the LORD has said to you, "You must never return that way again." [17]And he must not acquire many wives for himself, or else his heart will turn away; also silver and gold he must not acquire in great quantity for himself. [18]When he has taken the throne of his kingdom, he shall have a copy of this law written for him in the presence of the levitical priests. [19]It shall remain with him and he shall read in it all the days of his life, so that he may learn to fear the LORD his God, diligently observing all the words of this law and these statutes, [20]neither exalting himself above other members of the community nor turning aside from the commandment, either to the right or to the left, so that he and his descendents may reign long over his kingdom in Israel.

The description of royal activity in this text makes us think immediately of Solomon as one who acquired many horses and many wives, as well as selling some of his people to foreign nations such as Tyre and Egypt. The biblical audience likewise made the connection with Solomon, who for them represented the evils of kingship, despite the fact that he gave them a temple and an era of national greatness. Solomon also was confronted by a prophet for his religious and social abuses. Commentators have suggested the circumscribed guidelines for a king in this chapter and in Deuteronomy in general indicate that the authors of Deuteronomy were more critical than the authors of the Deuteronomistic History (Joshua, Judges, Samuel, and Kings). Perhaps the law was written by reformers who looked back in frustration at so many kings who abused royal power.[4]

Some commentators intuit that additional royal practices may have been prohibited by this text, which were not explicitly mentioned. If a king cannot collect gold or silver, nor can he collect horses, it would seem that his war-making capacity was severely limited. Horses were used by cavalry, and they also pulled chariots, the ancient equivalent of a tank. At first glance one might think the horse reference was meant to restrict trade, but the allusion may have included a subtle condemnation of the royal power to wage war. The reference to gold and silver in this context alluded to the king's ability to hire mercenaries for his army and to offer payment to other countries to ally with him in war. The suggestive comment that the king should not return people to Egypt to obtain horses might have described trading relationships, or it might have referred to a more sinister activity of selling your own people as slaves in order to obtain money or horses.[5]

The allusion to many wives suggested covenants or pacts with foreign powers, since a treaty-making process always meant an exchange of princesses, who were by definition called the royal wives. If the king was limited in making treaties with foreign powers, this meant that he could not carve out military alliances in preparation for war. Hence, it is seems that the war-making capacity of kings was limited.[6]

We suspect that the reference to Egypt and horses may have referred to sending an Israelite army to help a foreign king, perhaps a veiled allusion to politics in the age of the Assyrian Empire in the seventh century B.C.E.[7] The Israelite or Judahite king could have sent his own people to die in another country for the sake of political scenarios not relevant to the defense of Israel or Judah, and this would have wasted their lives for the sake of money for the king. Even in our own age it is the ability of the president to engage in limited military strikes with emergency power that can give him tremendous power. By convincing the public that there is a national crisis, and then by bringing military force into play, the administration is able to convince people to voluntarily give up their freedoms and transfer more power to the administrative wing of the government. We saw this happen to a great extent in our war in Iraq and the greater struggle with world terrorism. If we say that we are fighting for democracy, is it not ironic that we surrender democratic rights in that struggle? In the ancient world the ability of kings to wage war also brought them booty and wealth and enabled them to strengthen their rule at home. War-making abilities give tremendous authority and power to the governmental leaders. Some things in history never change, do they?

If these laws in Deuteronomy 12–26 were first written down in the time of Josiah in 622 B.C.E., and if they were the "Book of the Law" discovered in the temple and read to Josiah, one can imagine the impact on that young king. He was chided not to imitate the actions of his ancestor and predecessor Solomon. Even more dramatically, he was admonished to have a copy of this law made for his own personal reading, so that he might be reminded of what constituted legal justice. The copy was made in the presence of levitical priests, perhaps to insure that the entire code was copied. Kings elsewhere in the ancient world would never have consulted a written law code like this, for kings were the supreme power of the land.

Even scholars cautious about attributing too much revolutionary thought to this passage acknowledge its ultimate significance for later developments. Some believe the law was designed merely to limit the power of the king so that he would not enter into foreign alliances in a subordinate status, such as being a vassal to Assyria, for that would place a heavy tribute burden ultimately on the peasants. But even if this is so, there was a concern for the condition of the peasants that took priority over the political agenda of the king.[8]

What is most amazing was the assumption that the king was subordinate to this law. In the ancient world kings portrayed themselves as the mediators of the law codes given directly to them by the gods; usually the sun god Shamash did this in Mesopotamia. Hammurabi was portrayed as receiving his law code from Shamash, and this gave the code special authority. In reality, the ancient kings were the authors of the codes, or they at least directed their scribes to generate these codes as a statement of their ability to rule the people with justice. In this biblical text, however, the law code came from God and was specifically binding upon the king. To be sure, Josiah, as the king, would have been responsible for the implementation of this law and its subsequent administration. To that extent he functioned in the same way as any ancient Near Eastern monarch. But there is that distinct difference that the law explicitly put particular limitations on the king, which was a radical idea. Such a notion of limiting royal power would become foundational for those early theorists of democratic thought in the seventeenth and eighteenth centuries during the Enlightenment.

Furthermore, an even more radical statement said that the king should not exalt himself above other members of the community, which implicitly said that he stood before divine law as an equal to other people. The power of this statement cannot be underestimated. It implied that not only was the king under the law, but he was equal to other Yahweh believers who also stood under the law of God. This resonated with other texts in the Hebrew Bible that spoke of such human equality.

If we observe the book of Deuteronomy as a whole, we sense that this law in Deuteronomy 17 was part of a greater political vision designed to trim the powers of the king. Other laws distributed political and religious authority to various other social institutions, including local courts (Deut 16:18; 17:2-7), a central court (Deut 17:8-13), Levites (Deut 18:1-8), and even prophets (Deut 18:15-22). Some of these assigned responsibilities normally were the prerogatives of kings. Of all these institutions and offices, only kingship was without divine mandate for its founding, and kingship also appeared to be an optional institution, since royal duties could be exercised by these other offices. Kingship was created, according to Deut 17:14-15, by the desires of the Israelite people to imitate the governance of other societies; it was contingent upon human desire, not sent down from the heavenly realm. In Mesopotamia documents like the *Sumerian King List* explicitly said that, for in the ancient Near East, the institution of kingship was at the heart of national polity, and other social institutions revolved around it. In Israel, kingship, according to Deuteronomy, was actually of lesser importance because it shared the power with other institutions, such as the Levites, the priests, and prophets. One can see this in various laws in Deut 16:18–18:22, which described the rights and prerogatives of other groups of people in society. There was to be a balance of power between all these people. In the laws of Deuteronomy kingship generally was a contingent institution and it held minor status in Israelite society.[9]

Some critical scholarship suggests that the format of the law code in Deuteronomy may subtly imply egalitarianism. Laws in the ancient world were symbolically seen as addressed to kings from the gods, and the kings subsequently presented them to the people. The laws in Deuteronomy 12–26 were addressed directly to the people through Moses the prophet, not a royal intermediary. People were addressed by these laws in second person verb forms, either in the second person plural (and that is logical) or the second person singular, which is strange if you are speaking to a crowd. Perhaps, the second person singular forms were used at times because that would be the form used by the god(s) to address the king. If so, then the people, escaped slaves, received the rhetoric once destined for the royal ears.[10] People usurped the place of the ancient Near Eastern king.

Within the Deuteronomistic History we can observe other texts that demonstrated a critical stance over against the ideology of kingship. As such they tell us that Deut 17:14-20 was not an isolated text, but it reflected an ideology in the minds of the Deuteronomistic Historians.

The speeches of Samuel in 1 Samuel 8 and 12 are recognized as editorial creations that reflect the theological agenda of the Deuteronomistic Historians. Like the law in Deuteronomy 17, they commented unfavorably on the absolute power held by kings, and they implied that a good king was one whose authority was limited by law and the prophetic word.

1 Sam 8:10-18 listed the bad things that kings do. The speech was portrayed as an address given by Samuel to dissuade early Israelites from seeking a king. In subtle fashion it rehearsed the activities that later kings, especially Solomon, undertook and thereby used to oppress people. The implication was that these things should not be done by just kings, and perhaps laws such as Deut 17:14-20 could prevent them. Samuel warned how a king would take young men and place them into the military (to die fighting superior forces of a foreign army), and he would take other young men to work his farms and make his war implements (to use them as virtual slaves). The king would take young women to be perfumers, cooks, and bakers in his palace (potentially to become objects of his sexual avarice). The king would seize produce from fields and vineyards, debt slaves from the people, and animals from the herds. Eventually even the free people would be reduced to debt slavery. This language clearly reflected the judgment oracles of the preexilic prophets, especially Amos, and it reflected the historical experiences of many people from the period of the Divided Monarchies. In 1 Samuel 12 Samuel gave his farewell address, which included historical memories and warnings. In particular, in 1 Sam 12:14-15, 20-25 Samuel warned the new king, Saul, and the people that God will punish them if they do not obey the law. Thus, king and people both stood under the law and the prophetic word. Obedience to the law will bring blessing; disobedience will bring divine punishment—to king and commoner alike. No mention was made of the king's ability to mediate and divert such punishment. Like the people, the king must obey the law also.

Both texts appear to be Deuteronomistic rhetoric designed to complement the law in Deuteronomy 17 that called for the limitation of the powers of the king. Such a rhetorical appeal was remarkable in the ancient Near East in the middle of the first millennium B.C.E. To say that the king was under the authority of the law and the words of the prophets was a revolutionary religio-political assumption in that age. The seventh- and sixth-century B.C.E. cry of the Deuteronomic reformers against the institution of kingship reminds us of the Greek revolt against city tyrants in the sixth and fifth centuries B.C.E. in mainland Greece and Ionia. "The Deuteronomic and Deuteronomistic concepts of an ideal society were the cradle for the modern world," especially "for the modern humanism of human rights, including equal rights of men and women," according to Eckart Otto.[11]

Our perception of the message found in Deut 17:14-20 and 1 Samuel is not an optimistic, egalitarian interpretation forced on the Bible by modern critical scholars living in a democratic age. No less a great author than John Milton saw clearly the message contained within these passages. In his political work, *The Ready and Easy Way to Establish a Free Commonwealth, and the Excellence Thereof Compared with the Inconvenience and Dangers of Readmitting Kingship in This Land*, Milton derived the following principles from a reading of these texts: (1) popular sovereignty, (2) individual liberty, (3) civil rights, (4) elected assembly, (5) small government, and (6) advancement by merit. Milton used these biblical texts for his political exposition because he was convinced that they had the power to liberate people.[12] We have not imposed modern values on the Bible when we discern egalitarianism within its pages; no, the Bible has after many centuries imposed its egalitarianism on us.

Finally, a modern author said it well concerning the laws in Deuteronomy, especially the law on kings, declaring the book to be "a social charter of extraordinary literary coherence and political sophistication" and "the archetype of modern western constitutionalism."[13]

5. The Moses Traditions

I

The narratives of Genesis, Exodus, and Numbers, were probably generated in written form during the sixth-century B.C.E. Babylonian Exile or later, but in oral form they may have preexilic origins. We consider them at this point, after reflection on the words of the prophets, because the accounts have taken final artistic form with authors who may have been familiar with the words of the prophets. Sometimes the story line in Exodus betrays hints of the needs faced by Jews in exile in sixth-century B.C.E. Babylon (i.e., when Moses confronted Pharaoh's magicians, the word used for magicians refers to Babylonian divinators elsewhere in the Bible).

Stories in the book of Exodus have been attributed to epic cycles known as the Yahwist and the Elohist. In recent years most scholars suppose that the Elohist accounts, formerly attributed to the tenth through the eighth centuries B.C.E., are merely fragments used by the Yahwist historian during the exile. I still suspect that the Elohist fragments, or "pools of oral Elohist tradition," may have had an independent existence in the seventh century B.C.E. in Israel and later in Judah before they were drawn into the sixth-century Yahwist cycle as well as into the seventh- and sixth-century Deuteronomistic History.[1]

II

In Exod 1:15-21 we read the account of the midwives who defied Pharaoh and refused to kill the Hebrew baby boys. Scholars assign this narrative to the epic cycle called the Elohist because of the affinity of this story and other accounts in Exodus with northern prophetic traditions in the books of Kings.[2] This powerful narrative certainly reflected the theological agenda of the classical prophets. The tyrant in this passage was called the "king of Egypt," not "Pharaoh" as in Yahwist epic material, for the author wished the audience to think of their own kings.

> [15]The king of Egypt said to the Hebrew midwives, one of whom was named Shiphrah and the other Puah, [16]"When you act as midwives to the Hebrew women, and see them on the birthstool, if it is a boy, kill him; but if it is a girl, she shall live." [17]But the midwives feared God; they did not do as the king of Egypt commanded them, but they let the boys live. [18]So the king of Egypt summoned the midwives and said to them, "Why have you done this, and allowed the boys to live?" [19]The midwives said to Pharaoh, "Because the Hebrew women are not like the Egyptian women; for they are vigorous and give birth before the midwife comes to them." [20]So God dealt well with the midwives; and the people multiplied and became very strong. [21]And because the midwives feared God, he gave them families.

This was an incredible story of civil disobedience. Two midwives, who might have been either Hebrew or even Egyptian, had the courage to defy Pharaoh. Midwives were counted among one of the lower classes of society, and Pharaoh in Egypt was accorded the title of god—the incarnate god Horus, son of Osiris. They were also women in a man's society. But the midwives "feared God" (v. 17), and this enabled them to have the courage to defy Pharaoh. Would that Christians in the past two thousand years might have had the fear of God to make them refrain from genocide! The fuller implications of the monotheistic (r)evolution still have not unfolded completely, especially in the hearts and minds of many Christians even in our modern era. (I refer to the emergence of the monotheism as both a revolution and an evolutionary process with words used above, for monotheism is a revolutionary breakthrough, but it has to develop its fuller implications over many years.[3]) The "fear of God," which led them to moral behavior, typified stories that come from the Elohist tradition.[4]

Their names are recalled for us—Shiphrah and Puah. Pharaoh has no name for us to recall; he is a nameless and faceless tyrant. How ironic that powerful Pharaoh had his will bent by two peasant women. They were named and he had no name, for they prevailed.[5] Throughout the story of the exodus nameless Pharaoh symbolizes for readers the tyrants of every age, the nameless beasts who oppress and kill helpless people with all the power that organized states can muster. But the midwives have names for the readers of every age. Though they were small and insignificant by human standards, though they were flotsam in the machinery of a great imperial state, they had names because they prevailed and they can inspire us. They saved the Israelite boys, and without them and their rebellion there would have been no Israel, not even for Moses to liberate. They have names because they are the individuals of any age who have the courage to stand forth and defy imperial states and powerful Pharaohs. They have names because to the biblical author their courage was worth recalling. In their act of disobedience against Pharaoh, Israel was born. They are remembered forever, and Pharaoh with all his glorious splendor and might remains nameless.[6]

Not only did the midwives disobey Pharaoh, they played him for a fool to his face. They slurred the ethnic identity of Egyptians before him when they should have been quivering with fear. Egyptian women were weak, they said, unlike the Hebrew women who gave birth and were quickly out in the fields working, so that the midwives could not find them. (Their strong newborn babies were probably making bricks, too!) For the biblical author to portray such arrogance in the persona of the women before the divine Pharaoh was remarkable for any culture in that ancient age. Furthermore, the king of Egypt was portrayed as a fool, for he believed the women. Secure in the delusion of his divine status, surrounded by his trembling and fawning advisors, undergirded by his imperial bureaucratic structures, he assumed that no mere mortal, especially a woman and a midwife, would dare lie to him. But then such is the nature of tyrants, according to the biblical text, for they are fools who wallow in the folly of their pretentious power.

Normally a ruling race, upon subjugating a less fortunate race, might decide to commit genocide against them. But if so, they should kill the females, who reproduce, not the males, who can be a labor source until they die, even after the women are gone.[7] Tragically, this has been the way too often that genocide is carried out. Sometimes the women are not killed, but are handled in a different fashion. In the former Yugoslavia in the 1990s women were the targets of group rapes as part of the policy of "ethnic cleansing." The oppressors attempted to destroy the race of the Bosnians by impregnating the women with babies holding a different ethnic identity, relying on the Bosnian condemnation of abortion to make their plan effective.

Many years ago I studied Old Testament under a seminary professor who came from Germany. As a young professor in Germany he had closely read and studied this story of the women who rebelled against Pharaoh. He realized that Israel was born in an act of rebellion because two simple women had the courage to defy the state and to do what they felt was moral—not to kill the baby boys. In his opinion the women were Egyptian, so that their act of rebellion was even greater, for they sided with the helpless foreigners against their own mighty ruler. In choosing civil disobedience, they chose to respect life. As a German he was raised to obey his political leaders in all matters, with fear and obedience, for leaders were wise and knew more than did the average folk. But the deeper meaning of this story inspired him to engage in actions of resistance against his own government, as he realized that his government's attempts to purify their country were evil. He ultimately became involved with Lutheran clergy and German generals in the famous bomb plot against Adolph Hitler's life, which failed. He was not caught, but Dietrich Bonhoeffer, his friend, was caught and executed. When he told us this story, our jaws dropped. We all knew about Dietrich Bonhoeffer's actions and death. We had no idea that this professor was also involved in the bomb plot. Apparently he never spoke of this to his German students, only occasionally to American students when he taught in this country. He told us that we Americans could understand this story better than most people because our nation was born in an act of revolution two hundred years ago. The Bible is a dangerous book. It can lead a quiet little university professor to go up against one of the greatest tyrants of all time, just as the little midwives defied mighty Pharaoh. I hope that he is correct in his belief that Americans can understand this story better than most.

Finally, we must remember that the account used the expression "king" not "Pharaoh," so that the biblical audience would sense that their own kings also received the brunt of this theological sarcasm. It is suggested that the Elohist tradition had a strong sense of obedience to God rather than kings and those in power. This would make the Elohist tradition an ethic of civil disobedience, a remarkable intellectual tradition to locate in the first millennium B.C.E.

III

The immediate cycle of Moses traditions had a subtle commentary on the nature of kings and the real presence of divine power. Moses' biography moved progressively through five stages: (1) he was born of slaves,

(2) he was raised in the palace, (3) he identified with the slaves and went to the wilderness, (4) he returned to the palace to confront the tyrant, and (5) he freed the slaves and took them to the wilderness where they found God on a sacred mountain. This narrative pattern reacted against what must have been a popular folklore pattern about a hero common in the ancient world. We suspect this because Sargon the Great, ruler of Akkad in Mesopotamia, told the pattern of himself in 2300 B.C.E. He was (1) born in the palace at the city of Kish, (2) exiled to the wilderness by being placed in a basket that floated in the Tigris River until he was saved, and (3) upon raising an army of Semites in the wilderness he returned to free the land of Sumer from the tyrannical rule of Lugal-Zagessi. Sargon's propaganda was used to enamor him to the Sumerians he ruled, since he was a Semite. The biblical author appropriated the baby in a basket motif and applied it to Moses to make a powerful theological statement. The biblical author added that Moses began life as a slave and ended his career leading slaves in the wilderness. Thus, Moses ultimately moved in the opposite direction of Sargon, from being a slave to prince and then back again to being with the escaped slaves. Moses became an anti-Sargon hero or leader.[8]

Most commentators are well aware of the similarity between Sargon's birth story and that of Moses, but often we overlook some interesting parallels between Moses and the Egyptian god Horus, which brought even greater irony to the narrative since Horus was symbolically equated with Pharaoh by Egyptians. Gary Rendsburg explicates these parallels brilliantly.[9] According to a famous Egyptian myth, recorded by Plutarch in *Isis and Osiris* and in the Papyrus Jumilhac, the god Seth or Set, the hippopotamus god, killed the good god Osiris, who then became the god of the underworld. But the wife of Osiris, Isis, was pregnant with Horus. She hid from Seth, gave birth to Horus, lovingly nursed him, and then hid him from Seth by placing him in a basket in the papyrus marsh. This is exactly what happened with Moses. While he was in the basket, Horus was guarded by the goddess Nephthys, who was his aunt. Ultimately Horus grew up and confronted and finally killed Seth after an eighty-year struggle. There are some interesting equations to be made with the Moses story: Seth is Pharaoh, Horus is Moses, Isis is the mother of Moses, and Nephthys is Miriam. The baby was saved by being hidden in the marshes from the evil person who sought to kill him. Eventually the baby came back to kill the evil personage. How ironic that Pharaoh, normally equated with Horus by Egyptians, became Seth in the biblical metaphor. Other striking and unique parallels include the following:

only in the Horus myth and the Moses story did the parents expose the baby at birth in order to protect him; only in those accounts was the decision made by the mother and the baby guarded by a female family member in the papyrus marshes. In both stories nursing was important, for Isis nursed Horus before exposure and the mother of Moses was presented to Pharaoh's daughter so that she then nursed Moses as a supposed nanny after Pharaoh's daughter adopted him. Moses was said to be eighty years old when he confronted Pharaoh, just as the struggle between Horus and Seth lasted eighty years. If, indeed, the biblical author cannibalized the Egyptian myth, this was a great polemic against Pharaoh. Moses symbolically became Horus, the patron deity of pharaohs, and Pharaoh became the evil god Seth. The biblical author took Egyptian mythology designed to undergird rulers and slammed it in their faces.

In my opinion the biblical author has used both the Sargon legend and the Horus myth. The biblical story also portrayed Moses like Sargon in distinction to Horus, in that both liberated people from an evil oppressor. Sargon freed the Sumerians, or so he said, from the Sumerian tyrant Lugal-Zagessi, and Moses freed the Israelites. Both Sargon and Moses were raised in a foreign land until they discovered their true identity and their destiny to oppose the evil king and free people. Both set up "rule" over the people they liberated. Of course, Sargon became yet another king, but Moses was the antiking by leading slaves in the wilderness. Nonetheless, it should be noted that the biblical author brilliantly crafted both the stories of Sargon and Horus together with his allusions. The biblical author portrayed Moses as the one destined to lead Israel out of slavery (Exodus 3–4), then further cast him in the romantic hero role as the child persecuted by an evil tyrant who later prevails over that tyrant as an adult.[10]

This motif of the exposed infant developed throughout the Moses traditions. Moses was exposed at birth as were so many other heroes: Sargon the Great of Akkad, Rama of the island kingdom of Ceylon in the epic narrative the Ramayana, Oedipus in the great tragedy written by Sophocles, and others. But what do all these other personages share— they are kings. Is Moses a king? He led people in the wilderness for a generation and ruled them. He dispensed laws to them that were given to him on a sacred mountain by Yahweh. Did not Hammurabi, the Amorite Babylonian lawgiver in the early second millennium B.C.E., provide laws to his people that were given to him from the sun god Shamash (at least that's what Hammurabi claimed in his inscription)? Moses appears as a king to us initially, but his kingdom was one of slaves, he led no worship in a beautiful temple, he had no palace, he wore no regalia, he possessed no wealth, and his retainers were few and humble in origin— Aaron, Miriam, and Joshua. His temple was a craggy mountain in the wilderness, and therein was the true God to be found, not in the posh palaces or ornate temples of settled society. Moses was not a real king by the world's standards; he was an antiking, or, better said, he was a true king by God's standards. But then neither was Yahweh a god by the ancient world's standards, for this deity lived not in the sacred temples of the great cities but in the wilderness, on a mountain, surrounded by slaves, served by a prophet wearing humble robes. Moses became the ultimate indictment of kings and rulers in this world and Yahweh provided that indictment. Marduk of Babylon and Re of Egypt had their powerful peoples of Mesopotamia and Egypt; Yahweh had slaves for followers. Whose people endure yet today?

The Moses traditions added two new stages—(1) Moses was born to slaves, and (2) he ultimately went with the people to find God in the wilderness. The typical hero tale would have the hero born of royal blood and exiled at birth so that, after the time of maturation in the wilderness, the hero returns to claim what is rightfully his and defeat the evil tyrant who exiled him and killed his parents. (He then marries the beautiful princess, lives happily ever after, and inspires Disney stories and *Star Wars* movies.) Home for the hero is the palace. But in the biblical story the hero's home was with slaves and ultimately with slaves in the wilderness at Sinai. For ancient Near Eastern people the abode of the gods was symbolically located in the "cosmic mountain," a Mesopotamian ziggurat or a grand Egyptian temple. For some ancients the abode of the gods would be the palace of the king. Both city temple and palace were the "navel" or center of the universe (depending upon your politics, whether you were priestly or royal in your sentiments!). But in this new narrative format the biblical author symbolically maintained that God was not found in the king's palace or the priests' temple in the urban centers of wealth and power. God was found in the wilderness at the only true "cosmic mountain," Sinai, and God was surrounded not by the powerful elite but by real people, freed slaves. The Moses narrative provided a continuation of the critique of kings found in Exodus 1. Again, in subtle narrative fashion a tremendous critique was laid at the feet of kings by the biblical author.[11] God sided not with the kings, but with the peasants, the broken and helpless people of this world, and the slaves. If you think about this long enough, it might make you a little uncomfortable to be a rich and affluent American in a world of poor and helpless people.

The birth narrative of Moses continued the theme begun with the story of the midwives. Mighty Pharaoh decreed that the baby boys were to be thrown into the Nile River—genocide was commanded (Exod 1:22). Scholars suspect this is a duplicate story. The account of the midwives was Elohist, but the narrative about tossing the babies in the river was Yahwist. In the former story the babies survived; the latter story is more brutal, for only Moses survived. Our final biblical narrative was crafted by an author who retained both accounts. The overall result was to portray Pharaoh as a persistently brutal tyrant and advocate of genocide in many forms. His goal was to eliminate forever the Israelites. The babies were killed presumably by "all his people," for the entire Egyptian populace was commanded to drown the little babies (Exod 1:22). How ironic that Pharaoh sought to drown the babies in the water, and someday those babies would escape while Pharaoh and his mighty host drowned in the sea crossing of the exodus (Exodus 14–15).[12] As Pharaoh was thwarted by the midwives, once again mighty Pharaoh was thwarted by two women, a mother and her daughter, both slaves, and, ironically, they succeeded with the assistance of Pharaoh's own daughter. Women saved the future of Israel. God has a great sense of humor. We read this touching account in Exod 2:1-10,

> [1]Now a man from the house of Levi went and married a Levite woman. [2]The woman conceived and bore a son; and when she saw that he was a fine baby, she hid him three months. [3]When she could hide him no longer she got a papyrus basket for him, and plastered it with bitumen and pitch; she put the child in it and placed it among the reeds on the bank of the river. [4]His sister stood at a distance, to see what would happen to him.
>
> [5]The daughter of Pharaoh came down to bathe at the river, while her attendants walked beside the river. She saw the basket among the reeds and sent her maid to bring it. [6]When she opened it, she saw the child. He was crying, and she took pity on him. "This must be one of the Hebrews' children," she said. [7]Then his sister said to Pharaoh's daughter, "Shall I go and get you a nurse from the Hebrew women to nurse the child for you?" [8]Pharaoh's daughter said to her, "Yes." So the girl went and called the child's mother. [9]Pharaoh's daughter said to her, "Take this child and nurse it for me, and I will give you your wages." So the woman took the child and nursed it. [10]When the child grew up, she brought him to Pharaoh's daughter,

and she took him as her son. She named him Moses, "because," she said, "I drew him out of the water."

The mother and sister of Moses acted with courage and cleverness. Their bold plan entailed risk. Placing the baby in the bulrushes of the river was dangerous, for the baby was exposed to the possible marauding of a crocodile or a hippopotamus. In such an event, Miriam, the sister, would have to plunge into the water and save the baby. (No, the baby was not sent down the stream randomly as the movie, *Prince of Egypt*, would have us believe. The mother and sister had far more concern for the baby than to desert him.) Picture, if you will, little scrawny, knobby-kneed Miriam splashing into the water and shouting with all her little might to frighten away the crocodile with its razor sharp teeth when it threatened baby brother sleeping soundly in his fragile little floating basket. Now imagine her years later standing next to her baby brother, once more by the water's edge, as the imperial war machine of Pharaoh and his chariots sank beneath the frothy, churning, splashing waves of the sea. Do you think she recalled with a sense of irony her childhood challenge to protect Moses and how the image of splashing water had come full cycle?

When Pharaoh's daughter found the baby, Miriam had to approach her with this offer of a wet nurse, which was a rather dangerous act again for Miriam. Slaves did not routinely approach royalty whom they did not know. Bringing the baby back to the true mother was also risky, for would not someone become suspicious about a small girl coming forward so quickly out of the river weeds to the princess with such an offer? The daughter of Pharaoh defied her father. She knew the baby was a Hebrew. She may have guessed who the little girl and the nursemaid really were. Let us not assume she was too stupid. But she protected the baby and thus defied the royal decree issued by her father to all Egyptians. Mighty Pharaoh was deceived in grand fashion by his daughter. This is great humor.

Pharaoh was played for a fool by three women, two of whom were slaves. Pharaoh or the tyrant of any age may exercise his royal power, but he can be undercut by the weak and lowly, and even someone in his own household. The weak and lowly have God on their side, and perhaps, in addition, Pharaoh was really stupid. The biblical authors loved stories in which the rich and powerful, especially kings, were defeated by the cleverness of the lowly. Altogether Pharaoh was defeated by five women in two stories. But it would only get worse for him.

We step back from the account and we see the little baby in the basket one more time. Here he lies in a basket in the water, the liberator of slaves, the man who will create Israel in the wilderness, the one through whom the Law will be given to humanity, a man whose image will tower over the Jewish tradition. Christians are immediately reminded of a comparable symbol in the New Testament—the baby in the manger who is God incarnate. In both stories there is a hint of the divine humor. What is small by the world's standard will ultimately conquer the world. Moses in the basket, floating on the water, is the ultimate antiking symbol.[13] He will survive in the water and thus defeat Pharaoh, and he will rule a kingdom of slaves that shall endure forever.

IV

The confrontation between the adult Moses and Pharaoh was dramatic, perhaps the most dramatic and prolonged interaction between two personages in the entire biblical text. It inspired Cecil B. DeMille to craft his movie *The Ten Commandments* in such stunning fashion, featuring the classic confrontation between Charlton Heston and Yul Brynner.

The biblical author likewise cast this confrontation in larger-than-life form, for the narrative not only portrayed the conflict of two powerful human representatives on the earth but also symbolized the conflict between Yahweh, the god of Israel, and the myriad gods of Egypt. Two passages make interesting references to Moses. In Exod 4:16 and 7:1 God said to Moses that he would be like a god before Pharaoh and Aaron would be his spokesperson to Pharaoh, which meant that Moses was god and Aaron was a prophet in this little drama. How interesting— Moses received temporary divine status in order to confront Pharaoh, who only claimed to be divine.[14] The plagues likewise symbolized the power of Yahweh to defeat the gods of Egypt, for many of the plagues attacked the power of Egyptian gods and unveiled their impotence or nonexistence. The Nile was a goddess; turning her into blood was a victory over her. It also insulted the creator god, Khnum, guardian of the Nile, and Hapi, the spirit of the Nile. Heket was associated with life and was symbolized by a frog's head; the death of the frogs greatly disturbed her. Bes was the guardian of the bedroom for Egyptians, and her domain was invaded by the frogs who fled the Nile. Hathor was imaged as a cow, Apis was the deity of sacred bull, and both were degraded when the cattle of Egypt were killed in two separate plagues. (Either they had

a lot of cows or the biblical author combined two separate plague traditions!) Seth, the protector of crops, failed in his job to protect the crops.
Destructive hail revealed the impotence of Nut, goddess of the sky. Casting darkness over the land for three days humbled the might of the sun
god, Re. Killing the firstborn usurped the power of Osiris, protector of
the firstborn. Throughout the plagues, Isis, provider of life and fertility,
must have been greatly distraught. We can see the Egyptian gods cowering in a committee meeting, wondering what blows will strike them
next.

The battle in the heavenly realm between Yahweh and the powerless
gods of Egypt was paralleled by the battle between Moses and Pharaoh.
These two men represented their gods, and Cecil B. DeMille captured
this symbol well when he had the defeated, and Reed Sea water-soaked,
Pharaoh declare to his leading lady that Moses' god was God, after she
had asked him whether he had brought back the head of Moses for her.
Yet in another way the two men were symbols for political reality. Pharaoh symbolized kings and all forms of tyranny, whereas Moses was the
leader of slaves, a people with no king save God. Moses was the nonking
leader of the slaves; he was the lawgiver. Law would replace the king.
Equality before the law would replace submission before the king. The
interplay of these two personages in our biblical text is the dramatic
conflict between tyranny and freedom, between kings and people without a king. The eighteenth-century American political authors and
preachers were quick to note these equations in the text in their sermons
and their flashing oratorical rhetoric.

Finally, Moses also confronted the magicians, who were yet another
extension of Pharaoh. With a sense of irony and humor the biblical author
unfolded the developing plot line of the plagues and wove into the narrative a clever series of snippets that spoke of how Moses confounded the
magicians in head-to-head encounters. In Exod 7:8-13 the competitors
stood before Pharaoh and threw down staffs that transformed into snakes.
Aaron threw his staff down first, then the magicians of Pharaoh did likewise, but the winner of the contest was the snake of Aaron and Moses
because it ate the other snakes—a tasty lunch. In Exod 7:14-25 the competition moved to water sports. Moses used his staff to strike the river water
and turn it into blood. Pharaoh's magicians did likewise, so Pharaoh went
to his house in a huff, presumably unimpressed with Moses' actions. But
how stupid of Pharaoh to do that, since the water remained transformed
blood and all the Egyptian people had to suffer polluted water. (I am reminded of the water polluted by industrial wastes along the lower Mis-

sissippi that comes forth from our taps and the seeming lack of indifference of governmental agencies to protect our vital lifeline. I am reminded of oil gushing into the Gulf of Mexico because of corporate incompetence of an oil company.) Where was Pharaoh, the great source of life and fertility, when his people had no water to drink? In Exod 8:1-15 the next round dealt with amphibian control. Moses brought forth frogs from the river. (I guess they didn't like the blood in the water either!) Pharaoh's magicians also brought up frogs. But this time Pharaoh actually asked Moses to relent and send the frogs into the Nile River. I suspect that was because the frogs were in Pharaoh's house too (v. 3). Did I forget to mention that they were also in his bed (v. 3)? When kings and politicians are affected directly by the pain and suffering that the people endure, then they will act. The final contest involved insects. Exod 8:16-19 tells us that Moses turned the dust of the earth into gnats. The magicians dropped out of the competition at this point because they could not bring forth gnats. The magicians did not show up for the plague of flies (Exod 8:20-32) or the livestock pestilence (Exod 9:1-7) competition. Their last appearance was for the dermatological event (Exod 9:8-12) wherein Moses brought boils to all the Egyptians. The text laconically stated in v. 11, "the magicians could not stand before Moses because of the boils, for the boils afflicted the magicians." They sat out the rest of the plagues, at home presumably, treating their boils. We can only imagine where they had their boils. The competition was over; they were defeated. It must have been with a sense of humor that our biblical author included the narratives of Moses' competition with the magicians of Egypt. He defeated them, and thus he defeated an extension of Pharaoh. In this competition Moses proved that he was wiser than Pharaoh and more fit to rule. Ultimately, he took the people out into the wilderness and ruled them in the name of Yahweh. His competition reminds us of other stories where a Jewish boy in the court of a foreign king prevailed over the wise men and diviners of the king (Joseph and Daniel).[15] In all these narratives the ultimate target of critique was the foolish king who surrounded himself with impotent advisors.

In summary, our biblical author has crafted a brilliant narrative of conflict between Moses, the representative of God, and the forces of tyranny arrayed against them. Moses, acting as God's warrior, defeated the gods of the Egyptians, the magicians, and Pharaoh. But ultimately it was Pharaoh and his defeat that we wish to focus on in detail.

The confrontation begins in Exod 5:1 when Moses and Aaron declared to Pharaoh, "Thus says the Lord, the God of Israel, 'Let my people go, so that they may celebrate a festival to me in the wilderness.'" Pharaoh's response was that he did not know Yahweh, nor could he let so many people out of work. Pharaoh had construction deadlines to meet. He then ordered that the Israelites make bricks without straw, and so the Israelites had to forage for their own straw (Exod 5:6-19). In the typical manner of kings, tyrants, and totally unconcerned bureaucrats Pharaoh called the Israelites lazy for not keeping up their quota of brick production when time was lost searching for straw, and in addition he beat the Israelite supervisors for poor production output. The biblical text spent a goodly amount of time telling the story of Pharaoh's irrational demands on the people to keep up brick production. I am reminded of people today who declare that welfare recipients should get jobs, when those jobs would pay only minimum wage and still leave families mired in poverty. I also am reminded of a truck factory where I once worked forty years ago, where management doubled the required output of finished products, overloaded the ability of the assembly lines to produce machinery that worked, and then blamed the workers for shoddy work. Some things never change; workers are still made to look for straw.

In the second confrontation with Pharaoh and his magicians (Exod 7:8-13), Aaron threw down his staff to become a snake, the magicians of Egypt did likewise, and Aaron's snake ate the other snakes. Pharaoh's response was interesting to observe. He walked away silently to his house. Pharaoh ignored this sign as many rulers and politicians so often ignore the obvious needs of people when they pursue their own dogmatic policies.

Subsequent encounters of Moses and Pharaoh unleashed the plagues as Pharaoh adamantly refused to budge on releasing the slaves. First, the water was turned into blood (Exod 7:14-25), but "Pharaoh turned and went into his house, and he did not take even this to heart. And all the Egyptians had to dig along the Nile for water to drink, for they could not drink the water of the river" (vv. 23-24). Pharaoh was blind to the suffering of his own people. How often in our world do dictators spend their country's precious cash on military hardware while their people starve? How often does the United States sell those very weapons to those dictators? We are all blind to the suffering of the poor peasants in those countries.

Pharaoh tried to make a deal with Moses in two instances. In the second plague of frogs (Exod 8:1-15), Pharaoh agreed to release the slaves if the frog plague ceased. But when the frogs died, Pharaoh changed his mind and reneged completely on his promise. The fourth plague of flies (Exod 8:20-32) elicited a partial deal from Pharaoh in which the Israelites could go a short distance into the wilderness (v. 28), but once the plague was over, Pharaoh again changed his mind. One is reminded of King Richard's broken promise to the peasants in the 1381 uprising in England. One is reminded of modern political candidates, who, once elected, never keep their promises. We recall all the broken promises of rulers to their people throughout history.

The third plague of flies (Exod 8:16-19), the fifth plague of livestock disease (Exod 9:1-7), and the sixth plague of boils (Exod 9:8-12) saw no response forthcoming from Pharaoh as his people suffered. Presumably he sat in his palace somewhat shielded from the misery his people experienced, a response not unlike that of kings and rulers throughout the ages.

In the seventh plague of thunder and hail (Exod 9:13-35), Pharaoh appeared to make the grand concession. He said, "This time I have sinned; the Lord is in the right, and I and my people are in the wrong. . . . I will let you go; you need stay no longer" (vv. 27-28). Yet again, once the plague was over, he changed his mind. This was the point at which the long-suffering Egyptians should have impeached their ruler. Too bad they did not have that power. Too bad we have that power and sometimes fail to use it when we should. There are some mayors in major American cities over the past generation who should have felt the wrath of a public recall.

In the eighth plague of locusts (Exod 10:1-20) even Pharaoh's advisors encouraged him to meet Moses' demand (v. 7), and so Pharaoh agreed to let the adult Israelites go out into the wilderness to worship God, but the children had to stay (vv. 8-11). After the locusts hit, Pharaoh agreed to release the people, but once the plague abated, he changed his mind again (vv. 16-20). Do we sense the pattern of broken promises by now? I believe that this is a vicious satire on kings and rulers as well as a story about liberation of slaves. Political leaders are duplicitous to an incredible degree, especially if it means curtailment of their wealth and power.

After the ninth plague of darkness (Exod 10:21-29) Pharaoh agreed to their exodus (vv. 24-29) and told Moses that he never wished to see him again (vv. 28-29). Then, almost as an afterthought, we are told that Moses informed Pharaoh of the tenth plague, the death of the firstborn (Exod 11:1-10), and subsequently the impact of this plague was experienced (Exod 12:29-32), at which time Pharaoh ordered the Israelites out. By the time Pharaoh did the right thing to protect his people, it was too late; ultimate disaster had struck. I am reminded of politicians who will ignore environmental concerns, until it is too late for all of us. Such is the way of rulers and politicians, who care not for the needs of their people.

The entire narrative of the plagues unveiled the nature of Pharaoh's rule. The text repeatedly says that Pharaoh hardened his heart and that God hardened Pharaoh's heart. The tension between these two statements is seen by some as contradictory, by others as complementary. Christians have used these passages to argue about the nature of divine will, human free will, and predestination. This interesting debate, however, has obscured our attention to Pharaoh as a ruler. Look past the theological rhetoric of heart hardening and see the responses of Pharaoh for what they are. He was a powerful political leader who made irresponsible and brutal decisions. His actions oppressed foreigners and endangered the lives of his people. The biblical author did many things with this narrative, but I believe one of the biblical author's agendas was to unveil the actions of kings in their political decision-making process. The narrative unveils for us how leaders so often elevate self-interest and predetermined policy so as to hurt the people they rule. Pharaoh's activities recall the kings in the judgment oracles of Jeremiah. They vacillated back and forth between alliances with Egypt and alliances with Babylon until ultimately they destroyed their nation. I think the Exodus narratives have been generated with an eye to the political events of the final years of Judah. Royal dishonesty and vacillation led to the destruction of the people. Such is the way of kings.

V

The final chapter in the mighty struggle between Moses and Pharaoh, or between God and Pharaoh unfolded at the crossing of the sea. Moses led the Israelite slaves to freedom, but God did the fighting for them. The most significant recorded event in the Hebrew Bible was the exodus out of Egypt; it was for the Hebrew Bible what the resurrection of Jesus was for the New Testament, the ultimate act of salvation wherein God acted dramatically in history to save helpless human beings at the moment of their complete despair. The exodus story often is used by liberation theologians as a symbol of the struggle of the oppressed against rich and power oppressors of any age.[16] The dramatic moment of the exodus experience was the crossing of the sea, recorded in prose in Exodus 14 and in archaic poetry in Exodus 15. Exodus 15 has been called the Song of the Sea, and actually there are two archaic poems in this chapter. There is the Song of Miriam in Exod 15:21 and the Song of Moses in Exod 15:1-18. Both recount the same story of how Pharaoh and his host pursued the helpless Israelites, but how, in turn, God hurled Pharaoh and his host into the sea. Since the sea represented the ultimate forces of chaos for ancient peoples, God's ability to use the sea as the tool by which to destroy the Egyptians was testimony to the ultimate power of God.

The Song of the Sea is seen by commentators as the archetypal story by which to speak of "holy war," that is, the battle between God and the enemies of Israel, or those times when God came to save helpless Israel from their enemies. What is most significant about the Song of the Sea is that it was a battle report that clearly departed from the battle reports found on Egyptian and Mesopotamian monuments. In these other reports, the gods fought for the people, but they did so through the agency of the king and his troops. The glory belonged to the gods, but it secondarily belonged to the king, who was, by implication, semidivine or divine. Needless to say, all these ancient Near Eastern inscriptions had as their ultimate goal the attempt to praise the king, the general, and the great commander in chief. (As is always the case in human history, it is the poor peasant foot soldiers who really do all the dirty work.)

The biblical text ridiculed the rhetoric of such kings. The Song of the Sea portrayed the "army" of Israel as poor helpless slaves waiting to be slaughtered on the banks at the other side. God did all the fighting. God threw Pharaoh and his host into the sea—God's great slam dunk. There was no king to fight and defeat the power of Pharaoh. God used the sea to defeat Pharaoh. That is what is truly important—there was no king for Israel. The only king was Pharaoh, and he was the one defeated by the sea. The proud Pharaoh, who should be the one to defeat the power of chaos in some mythic and symbolic ceremony, was the one who went under the waves. Pharaoh, who called himself a mighty warrior god, drowned in the sea, so that the gods of Egypt did not prevail over the chaotic waters, as the myths would have it, but were defeated by them.[17] The committee of Egyptian gods, who were licking their wounds over the plagues and wondering what could be worse, realized that this was worse—Pharaoh symbolically was dead. Biblical literature undercut the great military war imagery of the day. God fought in battle against the enemy, but God did it all without the agency of any king. This was yet again a great put-down of kings, but it was done by not mentioning any such figure in the narrative. The Song of the Sea perhaps became the template for other narratives of battle in the biblical text, which likewise stressed how God did all the fighting, especially a narrative like Judges 5, the story of Deborah and Barak in contest with General Sisera of Hazor.[18]

VI

Once the Israelites were symbolically freed from Pharaoh after the sea crossing, we see a new set of images presented to us in the wilderness traditions of Exodus 16–19 and Numbers 11–36. The people in the wilderness complained, and we speak of the Murmuring Traditions throughout these narratives. They complained about the lack of food, so they got manna and quail; they complained about the lack of water, so they found water from rocks; and they complained about Moses' leadership. One would think that the spectacular nature of the exodus experience would have taught them to trust God completely. No, they complained.

The real question is not why they complained, but why the biblical author included these stories. They were included because they described the people of any age who complain and overlook the blessings of God. These complainers longed to return to Egypt. How absurd for them to think that way. But our biblical author presented these people as a symbol of folks who fear the freedom of the wilderness and long for the absolute security of slavery. People often seek security over freedom, and the biblical authors sought to unveil that mistake. We can hear the biblical text say to us that if we are free, we must take responsibility for our freedom and make our own way in the wilderness. The man and the woman in the garden in Genesis 3 refused to take responsibility for their actions, blaming each other, blaming the snake. The Bible hits us hard on that theme—if you are free, you must take responsibility for your actions.

Another image, which often escapes us, is the symbol of the manna and the quail as signs of royal provisions. In the ancient world the king or pharaoh was seen as the source of fertility and the force behind successful crop yields. In concrete terms, pharaohs and Mesopotamian kings were responsible for the upkeep of the irrigation systems that provided water to the farmers. So there was a direct connection between royal administrative responsibilities and crop yield. Without an effective irrigation system either Egypt or Mesopotamia would have fallen into famine and ultimately chaos. The Israelites were out in the wilderness, beyond the effective control of any king. But Moses, the prophet, was the substitute for the king. He was the representative of the people to Yahweh, and through Moses' agency Yahweh provided the people with manna and quail. We read in Exod 16:2-3, 13-15:

> ²The whole congregation of the Israelites complained against Moses and Aaron in the wilderness. ³The Israelites said to them, "If only

we had died by the hand of the LORD in the land of Egypt, when we sat by the fleshpots and ate our fill of bread; for you have brought us out into this wilderness to kill this whole assembly with hunger." . . . [13]In the evening quails came up and covered the camp; and in the morning there was a layer of dew around the camp. [14]When the layer of dew lifted, there on the surface of the wilderness was a fine flaky substance, as fine as frost on the ground. [15]When the Israelites saw it, they said to one another, "What is it?" For they did not know what it was. Moses said to them, "It is the bread that the LORD has given you to eat."

In this narrative we see the distinctive themes of how the people yearned for the days when they were slaves in Egypt. They declared absurdly that they had fleshpots, or meaty stew, when they probably had thin, pathetic broth. But, like all people, they romanticized the past when they were faced with challenges in the present. They feared the wilderness and its challenges; they feared freedom and the responsibilities that freedom brings; and they ultimately were like children who fear adulthood and long for the security of their dependent childhood.

Yahweh provided them food, and consequently life, in the wilderness. This was the role of kings in the ancient Near East: to provide fertility and a bountiful harvest as they fought back the forces of chaos and the wilderness that threatened the fertile land. Now in the wilderness, in the land against which kings must struggle for fertility, God gave a bountiful harvest. God was more powerful than any king when it came to providing food. The people did not need a king to provide them with food, they had God.[19]

VII

The Moses traditions have powerful images of opposition to tyrannical kings. The conflict between Moses and Pharaoh was a powerful dynamic of conflict between the hero (Moses) or antiking and the classic tyrant (Pharaoh). Normally in such an epic tale we would expect Moses to defeat and kill Pharaoh and become the new king, who is the good king, who marries the beautiful princess and lives happily ever after in Hollywood style. It did not happen this way. Moses led the Israelite slaves off into the wilderness where he functioned as a prophet and lawgiver. Kings were found in palaces in cities, not in the wilderness on craggy mountains. Moses gave them laws to live by, not royal authority. Moses and the slaves lived in the wilderness, the places that kings deplore and oppose. Our biblical author has given us the tale of Israel and its antiroyal rhetoric. It is no wonder that Cecil B. DeMille found this to be the great inspiration for an epic cinematic creation.

6. Deuteronomistic History I:
Premonarchical History

I

There are extremely dramatic texts that recall how prophets criticized the actions of kings in Judah or Israel. We find such narratives about prophetic personages in the Deuteronomistic History. Deuteronomistic History is a term modern scholars have coined to describe the biblical books of Joshua, Judges, 1 Samuel, 2 Samuel, 1 Kings, and 2 Kings, a series of works that we believe were written out of preexisting oral and written sources. The book of Deuteronomy, with the speech of Moses in chapters 1–11 and the corpus of laws in chapters 12–26, was generated to be a preface to this history. Deuteronomy articulated the theological and moral guidelines by which the people of Israel and Judah were evaluated in this grand historical narrative.

These historical narratives may have arisen with two or more editions in the late seventh and mid-sixth centuries B.C.E. The first edition may have arisen during the reign of King Josiah of Judah, around 620 B.C.E., and the second edition may have arisen in the Babylonian Exile around 550 B.C.E. This would explain why the book of 2 Kings appears to have two endings.[1] (Some European scholars believe that there were three editions, described as DtrG, DtrN, and DtrP, respectively, a basic narrative, a law-oriented revision, and a priestly revision, all dated loosely to the sixth century B.C.E.[2] Some American scholars believe that there might have been a prior edition around 700 B.C.E. produced under King Hezekiah that was later developed in 620 and 550 B.C.E. in second and third editions.[3]) Notice how there are seven books when you place Deuteronomy together with these six Historical Books. In ancient Israel they would have been in the form of scrolls; so there were seven scrolls, and seven was a sacred number.

These books related the national history of Israel. The books of Genesis, Exodus, and Numbers told the prehistory of Israel, focusing on the stories of the patriarchs in Genesis and the generation that Moses liberated from Egypt in Exodus and Numbers. Only with Joshua's entrance into the land and the subsequent settlement of the Israelites can we say that we have a national epic history. From that point onward Joshua, Judges, Samuel, and Kings told the history of the nation Israel and the later divided kingdoms of Israel in the north and Judah in the south. One could be tempted to call these books a national or a "political" history, if we use the word "political" in a loose, premodern sense. In these works we have a theological interpretation of Israel's history that spoke of Yahweh's relationship to the corporate people. It is not history in the sense that we write historiography; rather, it was a sermonic interpretation of important events in the life of the people, which recalled experiences and used them to provide a meaningful message or lesson to the age of the author. Ancient authors were not obsessed with recalling the exact details of events, they were far more interested in the meaning of those events and their religious or political implications. The book of Joshua spoke of the entrance of Joshua's people into the land of Palestine, Judges recalled the early chaotic conditions of the premonarchic era, the two books of Samuel spoke of the three kings of the United Monarchy (Saul, David, and Solomon), and the two books of Kings recalled the kings of the two little kingdoms (Israel and Judah) that arose after the disintegration of Solomon's empire.

Most of the stories seemingly spoke of kings, but closer inspection reveals that the biblical authors' concerns lay more with the prophets who spoke to those kings, or against them, as was so often the case. In the final analysis of the biblical authors only three kings were deserving of praise: David, Hezekiah of Judah, and Josiah of Judah. This tells us a great deal, for the bulk of the kings received a very critical evaluation by the biblical authors. Kings were excoriated especially for failing to devote themselves to Yahweh exclusively, for encouraging worship of other gods, and for not centralizing worship in the temple in Jerusalem. The Deuteronomistic Historians wrote from the perspective of monotheism, a belief held at the time when they composed their history, but it certainly did not represent the beliefs of most people prior to the late seventh century B.C.E. Most Israelites throughout their history were polytheists, revering Yahweh as the national deity, but holding other gods in high esteem and worshiping them for the particular benefits that they might provide, such as fertility of the land and the family. Such popular deities would have included El, Baal, and Asherah (who was the consort of El, then seen later as the consort of Yahweh by some folk). At best, some of those earlier Israelites might have been monolatrous, that is, worshiping Yahweh with fairly exclusive devotion but not denying the existence of the other gods. Thus, Elijah's call to worship Yahweh and not Baal did not mean that he denied the existence of Baal; rather, he called upon people to ignore Baal.

The historical kings thought they were not doing anything evil when they sponsored the worship of diverse deities; they assumed they were being politically wise by respecting the gods of the various constituent population groups that they ruled. Yahweh deserved significant attention for them because he was the national god, but he was not the only one who needed reverence for the sake of the nation's needs. (You had to diversify your divine stock portfolio to be a wise ruler.) Also, the kings who pushed the exclusive worship of God may have done so not because they were monotheists but because in time of crisis the elevation of the national god for the sake of protection was the wisest strategy. This could explain the actions of Hezekiah of Judah around 700 B.C.E. The Deuteronomistic Historians would not admit that about Hezekiah or Josiah, preferring to portray them as somewhat more monotheistic. Kings were condemned for many things, but the chief charge laid at their feet was failure to promote exclusive worship of Yahweh.

How amazing that a history of the national kings should be so negative about so many kings. It appears that the author relished telling us all about "the often sordid and sinful story of royal reality."[4] What nation normally would produce a national history that takes its royal leaders to task for their sins? This is not the way that annalists or authors wrote in the ancient world, but it is the way that the biblical authors wrote. It is the legacy they bequeathed to us, and perhaps it influenced our occasional tendency to be self-critical in history writing.

There is a distinctive theology in the book of Deuteronomy as well as the frequent editorial comments found in the six Historical Books. The Deuteronomistic Historians interpreted history from the perspective of their commitment to the laws of Yahweh and exclusive devotion to Yahweh, especially as expressed in the book of Deuteronomy. Scholars debate whether the Deuteronomistic Historians were radical monotheists, totally denying the existence of other gods. Most everyone agrees that the idea of absolute monotheism would emerge a century later in the Babylonian Exile, when Jews were surrounded by religionists who worshiped other gods. Monotheism is best expressed in the oracles of Second Isaiah, a nameless prophet in exile around 550 B.C.E., whose oracles are found in Isaiah 40–55. Deuteronomistic Historians may have been practical monotheists, who declared that the other gods should be ignored and only Yahweh is to be worshiped. Also, Israelites should keep the laws or the Torah, which calls for equitable treatment of poor and marginal people, women, slaves, widows, and orphans.

A covenant was made between Yahweh and the people at Sinai in which Yahweh gave the land to the Israelites and in return they would worship Yahweh exclusively and keep the law. If they broke the law, then they broke the covenant, and they would be conquered by foreigners and eventually lose the land. The curses and blessings for this human disobedience or obedience were articulated in Deuteronomy 27–28. We see the hints of this threat of punishment for sin in editorial sections of the historical narratives such as Solomon's speech in 1 Kings 8. Historical memories were told as a sermon that declared that when people keep the law of Yahweh, they will be blessed in the land, but if they break the law, they will be punished. Hence, in the book of Judges every foreign invasion was seen as punishment for sin. But if the people repent, they will be forgiven, and Yahweh will inspire a deliverer who will save them from their enemies. The entire history was very preachy and often hearkened to how repentance will bring restoration of the relationship with Yahweh.

In one sense the Deuteronomistic History was written to explain why Israel and Judah were conquered and destroyed by foreign powers. The northern state of Israel was crushed by Assyrians in 722 B.C.E., and the southern state of Judah experienced the same fate in 586 B.C.E. at the hands of the Chaldean Babylonians. The Deuteronomistic History was interested in the destruction of Judah and the fate of the exiles of Judah in Babylon: it declared that Yahweh, their God, let them be defeated and exiled, but it also offered the subtle hope that if they repent of their sins, worship Yahweh exclusively, and keep the law, they will be restored. The actual return of exiles from Babylon to Palestine in 539 B.C.E. ensured that the Deuteronomistic History would be received by these people as authoritative Scripture forever.

This grand history traced the life of Israel from the time of Joshua's entrance into the land of Palestine until the release of King Jehoiachin from a Babylonian prison in 561 B.C.E. The history spent much time on the reign of David, and the prophetic careers of Elijah and Elisha.

II

One way to criticize kings in the Deuteronomistic History, as well as in the epic narratives in Genesis, Exodus, and Numbers, was to omit references to kings when we should expect them or when we would find them in comparable annals of other ancient peoples. Other ancient cultures spoke of their national origin concurrent with the emergence of the first king. The founder of the people of Israel was Moses, the great lawgiver, who was not a king. Usually in the ancient world lawgivers and founders of nations were kings. The subsequent story of the conquest told of the leadership of Joshua bringing the Israelites into the land of Canaan. The book of Joshua symbolically presented him as though he founded the political entity of Israel, and his conquests were symbolically described as though he conquered all of the land. He did not. In fact, David really unified the country years later. But Joshua was presented as though he were the founder of the political entity, and in the minds of some scholars the Joshua narratives portray him to contrast with David. Joshua was not a king! The book of Judges told many exciting stories of early leaders in Israel. None of them were presented as kings (except for Abimelech, who was a miserable failure as a king). The personage who occupied the biblical author's attention in 1 Samuel as leader of the Israel was Samuel. He was a prophet, not a king.

Thus, we should take note that the great founders, Moses, Joshua, and Samuel, were not kings. Two of these personages, Joshua and Samuel, were recalled for us by the Deuteronomistic History. This is the critique of silence. Even though the need for kingship was admitted in the book of Judges, nonetheless, the biblical historians gave examples of great leaders who were not kings.

Of course, since we are modern people, we may not notice that kings are missing in accounts where other ancient peoples would expect them to be. We have not really been too keen on the concept of kings and kingship in the past few centuries! Ancient people would expect great military accounts to praise the gods for acting on their behalf in defeating their enemies, but they would expect the agency of that divine activity to be the king. Ancient inscriptions gave credit to the gods for victory on the battlefield, but the person who did the speaking in these inscriptions was the king. Be it Ramses II of Egypt or Tukulti-Ninurta I of Assyria, both who lived only a short time before the emergence of Israel, the ruler was the one who praised the gods, for the gods acted through him to defeat the enemies. The exploits of the king were praised, sometimes to extreme lengths, as with Ramses II's inscription about his victory over the Hittites at the battle of Kadesh in Syria in 1286 B.C.E. This was the case with these inscriptions, even if, in reality, the king performed no actual frontline combat at all (or if he lost the battle, as Ramses II actually did).

In Israel, however, God did the fighting, and the exploits of the human heroes were minimized. Joshua was portrayed as God's prophet or servant, while God did the serious work. At the battle of Jericho in Joshua 6, God did all the fighting. The Israelites paraded around the city walls of Jericho, blew their trumpets, and then the walls fell down. (I've listened to bands that could do that!) Not much room here for a king to boast! God did it all. In fact, the entire book of Joshua continued this theme. The message was that kings were not really needed for leadership, only God.

In Judges 4 Deborah and Barak, the prophetess and the general, fought against Sisera, the general of Hazor, and the story was briefly recounted in a way as to leave no doubt that God won the victory. In Judges 5 a victory hymn of this battle was recalled in very archaic Hebrew. The song praised the victory of God in defeating Sisera and his forces, and no king or comparable figure for Israel was mentioned, not even general Barak.

In these biblical war accounts a deliberate criticism of kings may be seen, simply because the accounts left out the references to human heroes, kings, or generals, that the ancients would have expected.[5]

III

The book of Judges rendered an ambivalent message about kings. On the one hand the book indicated that prior to the emergence of kingship there was chaos in the land because there was no centralized rule (Judg 17:6; 18:1; 19:1; 21:25). In fact, the book concluded with the account of the rape of the Levite's concubine, the destruction of the tribe of Benjamin, the reconstitution of the tribe of Benjamin by the destruction of Jabesh-Gilead, the abduction of women from Shiloh, and these were all scandalous events. After these appalling accounts the final sentence in the book (Judg 21:25) cast judgment on the moral chaos, "In those days there was no king in Israel; all the people did what was right in their own eyes." The implication, of course, was that kingship was necessary for the sake of simple moral and social order in society. On the other hand, the book contained narratives and references that implied the evil nature of kings and the folly of creating a king. It may be that the book of Judges has been edited by at least two authors, one promonarchical and the other antimonarchical. We shall pay close attention to those accounts that contain the antimonarchical rhetoric.

In Judg 1:11-21 the tribe of Judah and other groups of people conquered land in southern Palestine, in what would become the tribal area of Judah. In vv. 5-7 the defeat of king Adoni-bezek was recounted. When he was captured, the Judahites cut off his thumbs and big toes. In v. 7 Adoni-bezek responded, "Seventy kings with their thumbs and big toes cut off used to pick up scraps under my table; as I have done, so God has paid me back." Including this quote in the history was a rather strange literary ploy by the author, unless the author intended to reflect upon the nature of brutal kings and the just reward they should receive. Such a punishment could be seen as an example of the humbling of royal pride in a "legend of derision."[6]

In comparable fashion King Eglon of Moab was assassinated by the judge, Ehud, in a grossly disgusting fashion, when Ehud stuck a knife into his overly fat stomach and his bowels exploded (Judg 3:12-30). This was a humiliating way for a king to die, and the biblical author seemed to take delight in it by including the account in detail. In fact, there may be more that needs to be said about this particular odd little narrative.

There are a number of narratives, which at first blush do not seem to criticize kings directly but, when we reflect upon the ancient understanding of kings as divine, these accounts present us with abrasive ridicule of kings as weak and even subject to overthrow by ordinary people. Some of these narratives portrayed foreign kings as totally ineffective before the heroes of Israel, and so they functioned as nationalistic tales used by the biblical authors in glorifying God, who defeated Israel's enemies. We also sense there was ridicule of the institution of kingship in these tales.

Eglon, king of Moab, invaded and ruled at least part of Israel for eighteen years with the aid of Amalekites and Ammonites. He ruled as king in the city of Jericho. The name Eglon came from a Hebrew word, "GL," which meant "young bull" or "fatted calf." This could not be his real name. His name foreshadowed his death. Ehud killed Eglon by driving a knife into his stomach or intestines while Eglon was sitting on the toilet having a bowel movement. Because Eglon was so fat, the left-handed Ehud had to ram the knife completely into his belly. Truly, a fattened calf ready to be butchered comes to mind with this graphic portrayal of Eglon's death. Ehud took him by surprise, for his weapon hand was his left hand, not his right hand. Eglon received tribute from Ehud, and when Ehud said that he had a message from God for Eglon, Eglon awaited it eagerly. He got his message—a knife in his stomach. What a completely humiliating way for a king to die, and what a brutally ironic title, "Eglon," to attribute to him. He was just a fattened calf waiting to be slaughtered, and Ehud was a commoner, an ordinary Israelite, who overcame the power of this conquering king.[7]

In Judges 4 Deborah and Barak defeated general Sisera, who fought for Jabin, king of Hazor. The narrative recounted not the battle but an incident after the battle. Sisera fled and demanded sanctuary from Jael the Kenite, and while he slept in her tent, she drove a tent peg through his forehead (Judg 4:17-22). The ignominious death of the general foreshadowed the later defeat of Jabin, the king (Judg 4:23-24). Perhaps the humiliating death of his general was meant to be a symbol for his own humiliating demise.[8]

The author of the book of Judges delighted in the superficial understanding of a quote by Gideon in Judg 8:23. After two delightful tales of how God called Gideon with the sign of the wet fleece and the dry fleece (Judg 6:11-40) and how God winnowed Gideon's troops down to three hundred soldiers (Judg 7:1-23), then we encounter stories of serious combat, which appear to be more like a historical memory of a battle (Judg 7:24-25; 8:1-21). After these victories the Israelites asked Gideon to be their king in Judg 8:22, and his response was important for the author, for Gideon declared in Judg 8:23, "I will not rule over you, and my son will not rule over you; the Lord will rule over you." The text became an example of how God should be Israel's king and not a human being. Indeed, this would be the understanding of many Jews after the destruction of Jerusalem and the end of kingship in 586 B.C.E. Postexilic psalms lauded the kingship of God in that age when Jews had no king of their own but were ruled by foreign nations.

If we read the narrative closely in Judges 8–10, however, we sense that the historical experience of Gideon might actually have been otherwise. His son, Abimelech, had a name that means "my father the king." Why did Gideon give him that name unless Gideon was perceived to be a king? Why did Abimelech try to become king himself in Judges 9–10, unless he believed he had the right of succession to kingship? Gideon may have piously said that God would be the real king, and that he would be the agent through whom God ruled. That would be a pious and gracious way to accept kingship. The fact that Gideon made an idol for the people to worship (Judg 8:24-27) makes us pause and think perhaps Gideon was performing some royal function in establishing this cult of the ephod. It appears that Gideon was the first person to become king over Israel, but his dynasty collapsed with his son, Abimelech. So our biblical author glossed over that historical memory and preferred to view Saul's kingship as the first attempt at kingship, which failed and was succeeded immediately by David's. By glossing over the memory of Gideon's real rule, our present biblical text now seems to focus on Gideon's supposed rejection of kingship. As such, it becomes another critique of kings.

Some commentators think that the account does condemn the kingship of Gideon, although in subtle fashion. If we compare Gideon's actions to the law about kings in Deuteronomy, Gideon appears to be condemned quite dramatically. During the battle Gideon inspired the men by crying, "For the LORD and for Gideon" (Judg 7:18). He should not have inspired the men to fight by invoking his own name if Yahweh were indeed the source of the victory. He took brutal revenge on the leaders of the two cities, Succoth and Penuel, because they would not help him in the mopping up operations (Judg 8:4-17). He killed the two enemy kings, Zebah and Zalmunna, when they were his prisoners (another humiliating end for so-called kings), but then he took for himself their crescents, which must have been religious and therefore idolatrous objects (Judg 8:18-21). Gideon then collected gold from the people (Judg 8:24-26), thus violating the guideline in Deut 17:17 about gold accumulation. He made an idol, which Israelites worshiped and "prostituted themselves" (Judg 8:27), thus violating Deut 17:20. Gideon had two names, Gideon and Jerubbaal (Judg 8:29); the latter was a Baal name. He had many wives (Judg 8:30), which violated Deut 17:17. He named his son Abimelech, which meant, "my father the king." What has been remembered in our narrative made Gideon look like a king, and one who violated the guidelines of kingship according to Deuteronomy 17.[9] Maybe our biblical author wished to have it both ways. The expression in which Gideon appeared to reject kingship became important for the overall story of the judges, yet at the same time Gideon was subtly condemned for acting as an unjust king by Deuteronomistic standards.

In Judg 9:1-57 we read how Abimelech, the son of Gideon, attempted to make himself king over Israelites. (His name either indicates that his father was king or that Abimelech wished people to think that Gideon was king.) Abimelech killed seventy of his brothers to ensure his hold upon the throne. But Jotham, the youngest, escaped and uttered a parable (Judg 9:7-15) and a sermon (Judg 9:16-20) as an abrasive critique of Abimelech's kingship. In his parable the trees sought to find a king to rule them, but after being turned down by the olive tree, the fig tree, and the grape vine, the lowly and worthless bramble bush (Abimelech) accepted rule and then threatened to spew forth fire. Such was the ridicule of Jotham not only for Abimelech, but also for the king-making process and kings in general. The parable reads as follows in Judg 9:8-15,

> [8]The trees once went out to anoint a king over themselves. So they said to the olive tree, "Reign over us." [9]The olive tree answered them, "Shall I stop producing my rich oil by which gods and mortals are honored and go to sway over the trees?" [10]Then the trees said to the fig tree, "You come and reign over us." [11]But the fig tree answered them, "Shall I stop producing my sweetness and my delicious fruit, and go to sway over the trees?" [12]Then the trees said to the vine, "You come and reign over us." [13]But the vine said to them, "Shall I stop producing my wine that cheers gods and mortals, and go to sway over the trees?" [14]So all the trees said to the bramble, "You come and reign over us." [15]And the bramble said to the trees, "If in good faith you are anointing me king over you, then come and take refuge in my shade, but if not, let fire come out of the bramble and devour the cedars of Lebanon."

This parable can stand on its own with meaning apart from the narrative in which it is found. You do not need to know the references to the aspirations of Abimelech to be king and how he killed all his brothers and half-brothers, save Jotham, the one who crafted the fable. The critique of kingship is clear simply within the parable itself. The power of the critique is carried by the humor of the story. The olive tree, fig tree, and vine all see their everyday function as more important than being king over the trees. What does this say about kingship in general? These plants view the institution as rather worthless. Only the pathetic bramble is willing to be king, and he is worthless. Perhaps only worthless individuals become kings, the parable implies. The pomposity of the bramble entertains. "Take refuge in my shadow" says the bramble. How paltry is the shadow that can be cast by the scrawny bramble. Further, the bramble declares, "let fire come out of the bramble and devour the cedars of Lebanon." Imagine a tiny bramble bush sprouting fire, and then imagine this fire destroying the most majestic trees known to the biblical audience. This is true sarcasm of kings and the pompous pride with which they comport themselves.

Commentators view this passage as the most abrasive criticism of the institution of kingship in the Bible and the ancient world.[10] Martin Buber, in particular, calls this the "strongest anti-monarchical poem of world literature."[11]

In the fable the reference to "shadow" alluded to the Egyptian and Mesopotamian imagery that spoke of the shadow of the king as a symbol of royal protective power extended to his subjects. The Jotham fable turned royal imagery upside-down by implying that the notions of protection and fruitfulness provided by the king do not exist.[12] Olive trees, fig trees, and vines are fruitful; brambles are weeds. Such was the nature of a king; he is a weed, totally without fruit for his people.

IV

Prophets stood in judgment over the kings throughout the rest of the Deuteronomistic History. Kings who were good heeded the words of the prophets, who spoke their word from the Lord. Ultimately, placing the book of Deuteronomy, with its law limiting the power of kings, at the beginning of the Deuteronomistic History, put kings not only under the prophetic word from the Lord, but also the Torah of the Lord.

7. Deuteronomistic History II: The United Monarchy

The story of the United Monarchy was recounted in the books of 1 and 2 Samuel. Many different sources have been woven together by the Deuteronomistic Historians to create this narrative, and sometimes these different sources were already highly theological and had different perspectives. Hence, modern scholars sense tension between the messages of the different sources. Some texts spoke positively about kings and others were negative. We notice specifically that royal annals about the deeds of David and Solomon, which by their very nature affirmed the accomplishments of those kings, were combined with negative observations, perhaps from the Deuteronomistic Historians themselves, which ultimately created an overall critical perception of the institution of kingship.

In 1 Samuel 1–15 a number of traditions have been brought together to tell how kingship first arose in Israel. Critical scholars suggest that four significant segments of literature have been woven together by the Deuteronomistic Historians: (1) The Samuel Idyll, 1 Samuel 1–3, contained old prophetic traditions about the little boy Samuel who functioned as a prophet at Shiloh in the midst of corrupt priests under Eli. (It also may be a synthesis of various traditions.) (2) The Ark Narrative, 1 Samuel 4–6 (also including 2 Samuel 6) was an account of how the ark of the covenant was lost in battle to the Philistines but was returned by them because of the damage it caused to their idols and their physical health. (3) The Promonarchy Source, 1 Samuel 9:1–10:16, 11, 13–14, was an old source that portrayed Saul as a charismatic hero who rose to be king by virtue of military prowess against Ammonites and Philistines, while Samuel was a local seer who anointed him to be king. (4) The Antimonarchy Source, 1 Samuel 7–8, 12, 15, was probably a late set of texts, maybe created by the Deuteronomistic Historians, designed to denigrate Saul, the king, in favor of Samuel, the prophet, who was most responsible for making him king and unmaking him king when he failed to heed the prophetic advice. The final overall message of the narrative was created by the antimonarchical texts that downplayed the power of the king before the role of the prophet, a message reflecting the view of biblical theologians after years of royal misrule in Israel and Judah.

The traditions about Saul in 1 Samuel 1–15 also portrayed Saul in a negative light in order to legitimate David's ultimate seizure of the throne from Saul and his family. The result, however, was a negative reading of kingship in general. These chapters provided ammunition to writers in the modern era to rail against the tyranny of kings, especially among eighteenth-century authors in America.

II

At the beginning of this narrative sequence we encounter the Samuel Idyll, which perhaps came from the northern prophetic circles that were critical of kings. Even at his birth the prophet Samuel stood in judgment over Saul, for he stole Saul's name. The long-suffering, childless Hannah finally received a son from the Lord, and in 1 Sam 1:19-20 Hannah named him Samuel because she "asked him of the Lord." Apparently Hannah did not know Hebrew or our biblical author had a sense of humor. Samuel (*Shmuʾel*) meant "name of God." "Asked of the Lord" alluded to the name of Saul (*Shaʾul*). Our biblical author intended this little joke to have a serious meaning, for Samuel made Saul king, and Samuel rejected Saul as king. The prophet of the Lord had final say over the king. Hence, at his birth Samuel already demonstrated his authority over Saul by stealing Saul's name for himself. If the first king was under the guidance of a prophet, were not all kings subordinate to prophets?

When the people sought a king to physically rule over them, the adult Samuel warned them of the folly of this decision. Samuel prayed to the Lord, and he received a divine response 1 Sam 8:7-9:

> ⁷Listen to the voice of the people in all that they say to you; for they have not rejected you, but they have rejected me from being king

over them. [8]Just as they have done to me, from the day I brought them up out of Egypt to this day, forsaking me and serving other gods, so also they are doing to you. [9]Now then, listen to their voice; only—you shall solemnly warn them, and show them the ways of the king who shall reign over them.

What was truly powerful about this divine speech was that the Lord declared that in seeking a king, the people have rejected the Lord (v. 7). In the ancient world kings were seen as the divine extension of the gods, a representative of the gods, even a god incarnate, and kings acted out the will of the gods on earth. Here we have the incredibly radical political statement that the desire to have a king was a rejection of God. Furthermore, God took the opportunity to allude to the rebellious activity of the Israelites in the wilderness, further casting aspersions on the whole institution of kingship. God, in fact, even told Samuel to warn the people what they have in store with the arrival of kings. So in the following verses Samuel warned them and, indeed, predicted what would come. His speech was located in 1 Sam 8:11-18:

> [11]He said, "These will be the ways of the king who will reign over you: he will take your sons and appoint them to his chariots and to be his horsemen, and to run before his chariots; [12]and he will appoint for himself commanders of thousands and commanders of fifties, and some to plow his ground and to reap his harvest, and to make his implements of war and the equipment of his chariots. [13]He will take your daughters to be perfumers and cooks and bakers. [14]He will take the best of your fields and vineyards and olive orchards and give them to his courtiers. [15]He will take one-tenth of your grain and of your vineyards and give it to his officers and his courtiers. [16]He will take your male and female slaves, and the best of your cattle and donkeys, and put them to his work. [17]He will take one-tenth of your flocks, and you shall be his slaves. [18]And in that day you will cry out because of your king, whom you have chosen for yourselves; but the LORD will not answer you in that day."

This text dramatically described the many things that were done by Solomon (1 Kgs 4:22-28; 10:14-29; 11:1-13).

One commentator describes this text as politically subversive, for it undermines the entire notion of kingship as an important and necessary human institution, implying instead that commitment to God alone provides sufficient grounding for a nation's political identity.[1] Another modern author points out that this narrative implied that kingship arose because of an act of disobedience on the part of the people—they essentially rejected the rule of Yahweh in the editorial opinion of the biblical writers.[2]

A good example of the subversive nature of this passage may be found in the work *Common Sense* by Thomas Paine. Paine vociferously condemned the institution of kingship and called on Americans to seek political independence from England. For two pages in his brief pamphlet Paine attended to a discussion of 1 Samuel 8 as the best example wherein the Bible condemned the "idolatrous" institution of kingship. Paine's discussion focused on this passage more than any other biblical text. Paine's essay was instrumental in convincing a large number of American colonials that they should seek complete independence from England.[3]

Scholars have argued whether the language of this passage reflected insights from early in Israel's monarchic history or whether it came after centuries of bad experiences with kings, perhaps from the late seventh century B.C.E. The date is not really relevant for the theological significance of this passage. Either way the text emanated from the first millennium B.C.E. and was significantly advanced over contemporary beliefs in the ancient world. In fact, its critical indictment of kingship was more advanced than European thought until the last four centuries.

Nations of the ancient world spoke of how kingship was a gift of the gods. The *Sumerian King List* declared that kingship descended from heaven. The ancient third-millennium B.C.E. Sumerian myth of *Etana* spoke of how kingship was stolen from the divine realm. Here the biblical text made it quite clear that people in a moment of sheer folly asked for kingship, and they got it. What greater sarcastic ridicule of kingship could the biblical author present?

Saul undertook military action that led to his emergence as king when he marshaled Israelites to go forth in war to save the city of Jabesh-Gilead from Ammonite takeover (1 Samuel 11). Saul heard that the Ammonites demanded the surrender of the people of Jabesh-Gilead with the corollary that as prisoners they must submit to having their eyes gouged out so as to render them unfit to fight effectively. In a rage he cut up an oxen into twelve parts (1 Sam 11:7) and sent it to the various tribes, declaring that whoever did not come out to fight would be cut up in similar fashion. That was quite a threat to give to people he sought to recruit. But it reminds the listener or the reader that in Judg 19:29-30 a Levite cut up his dead concubine and sent the parts to the other tribes to bring them forth to war against the tribe of Benjamin for the sexual assault in the city of Gibeah. Since Saul was from the tribe of Benjamin, his action in cutting up the oxen reminds us that he comes from a tribe that had done evil in the past. That was a little editorial trick by the final author of this biblical text to discredit Saul.[4]

When Saul defeated the Ammonites, who were besieging Jabesh-giliad (1 Sam 11:1-11), the Ammonite king was Nahash. Nahash means "snake." His name meant snake. This could be the real name of a king, who wished to inspire fear among his subjects, but possibly this was yet another name made up by the biblical author. The snake was sometimes equated with the chaos beast, who threatened world order and had to be defeated by the good god. In Israel Yahweh was said to have defeated Yam (the sea), or Rahab, or Tannin (a large snake). In Babylon the god Marduk was believed to defeat Tiamat, the chaotic goddess of water, with the coming of every New Year. Tiamat was portrayed as a seven-headed dragon or large snake. In Egypt the god Re was thought to defeat Apophis, the snake god of darkness, every morning. Thus, in 1 Samuel 11 the Ammonite king, Nahash, perhaps was symbolically equated with the symbol for the forces of chaos. Normally kings sought to identify with the deity who defeated the chaos beast; kings might even role play the warrior deity who defeated chaos in some dramatic performance during the New Year's celebration. How insulting it was to declare that the Ammonite king was to be identified somehow with the evil deity of chaos. He was defeated by an ordinary Israelite, Saul, who was led by the spirit of God. The narrative may not only have been a heroic account about Saul's early accomplishments, it may also have been a stunning critique of ancient kings.[5]

Saul was crowned king by Samuel three times (1 Sam 9:15–10:8; 10:17-24; and 11:14-15), which were probably different memories of his coronation. The biblical author included all three of them for several reasons, but they truly impress upon us that Saul, the king, was empowered by a prophet. It reinforced the image of the king's subordination to the prophet. The last account of coronation came after his great victory over Nahash, "the snake," and indicated his subjection to the prophet Samuel despite his recent great accomplishments.

Ultimately Saul found himself later criticized by Samuel, the prophet, but also disowned as king because he failed to obey Samuel's orders (1 Sam 15:1-23). Saul failed to kill all of the Amalekites and their cattle, so Samuel "unmade" Saul as king, just as he had "made" him. Important in this account and other Samuel narratives was the theological concept that prophets "made" kings and spoke an authoritative word to them. Elsewhere in the ancient world prophets might try to offer advice to kings, but they did not make them and disown them. Samuel chose both Saul (1 Sam 9:1–10:16) and David (1 Sam 16:1-23) according to the biblical author, because he had a commission from Yahweh to make these men kings. This was not a concept by which kingship in the ancient world generally functioned, but it was a theological belief found among the scribal intelligentsia who generated the Deuteronomistic History.

In addition, there seems to be some symbolism present in the story of Saul and Agag. In 1 Sam 15:1-33, after Saul defeated the Amalekite king, Agag, in battle, he did not kill him as the prophet Samuel commanded. When Samuel came to the battle camp and discovered Agag alive, he told Saul that God rejected Saul, and then Samuel cut Agag into pieces with a sword. Agag's name may have meant "fury" or "rage." Cristiano Grottanelli believes that the word is reminiscent of the Akkadian word *agagu*, used in the Assyrian *Epic of Irra* (750 B.C.E.) to describe the wrath of the god Irra, who visited destruction upon the world.[6] Perhaps, we again have a symbolic name used to describe a king, who was equated with a malevolent deity of destruction instead of the god who maintained order. Kings were to be like Marduk or Re and bring order and stability to their people and the world. Not Agag. Like Nahash, he was a god of chaos and destruction. Samuel carved him up in the same way that Marduk sliced Tiamat.

It is an interesting coincidence that the earlier story in Judges 3 about Eglon the Moabite said that he had Ammonites and Amalekites for allies. Then in 1 Samuel 11 Nahash the Ammonite was defeated, and in 1 Samuel 15 Agag the Amalekite was defeated and ultimately killed by Samuel the prophet. Grottanelli suggests that these three stories were told together and that perhaps they were recalled in the Israelite shrine at Gilgal. He notes that each of these three accounts stresses how Yahweh defeated an evil king, two of which are portrayed as monsters (he thinks it is true of all three). Significantly Yahweh accomplished this through the efforts of a common person, a warrior or a prophet. The three accounts shared the interesting theme of how the monster king was slain by a hero, and thus kingship was ridiculed. In their present form, two of these stories were reused by the biblical author in 1 Samuel 11 and 15 to relate victories of King Saul.[7] Ultimately, after reflection upon these three stories, I believe that the image of the common person slaying the evil king, who is also a monster, is not only a romantic image, it is a very democratic image. It leaves a subconscious impression in the minds of readers that perhaps tyrannical kings should be overthrown by the common folk.

After Saul was disowned and David secretly anointed as king in his place by Samuel, the text portrayed the disintegration of Saul. He slowly went mad and needed David to play music for him (1 Sam 16:14-23). Portraying a king as mad is something that people in any age might suggest, but to simply write it down in the national epic is rather stunning for an age that considered kings to be divine or semidivine. Saul deteriorated so much in his rage that he ordered innocent priests at Nob slain simply because he suspected that they were supporting David (1 Sam 22:6-30). With this bloody act he became the ultimate tyrant.[8] It is impressive that an ancient text would recall this particular act of brutality, especially since priests were considered sacred. Saul's insanity brought him to the final act of degradation—he consulted a witch at Endor to discern his future, even though he previously outlawed witches (1 Sam 28:3-25). Did not kings in the ancient world have access to divinators who could skillfully predict the future? Did not the kings of Israel have prophets to whom they could turn for advice? But Saul crept in the night to a dark practitioner of the black arts to discover his fate. Such is the destiny of the tyrannical king, who like Macbeth, must perish at fates unleashed by his own evil actions. Where is the wisdom of kings so lauded in the ancient world when we read this story? The demise of Saul told in the second half of the book of 1 Samuel was a striking account that unveiled the fallibility of kings.

III

In the books of 1 Samuel, 2 Samuel, and the beginning of 1 Kings we have the dramatic narratives of David, who, along with Moses, is one of the most important figures in the narratives of the Bible. When we read these accounts, many of which have inspired movies in the modern age, we see grand story lines of a young boy who became king, killed Goliath, survived Saul's attempts to kill him, used clever strategy to assume rule, survived the rebellion of his son Absalom, and, in general, turned the small little nation of Israel into a great and mighty power. We are so entertained and inspired by these accounts we fail to appreciate their subversive nature and how they undermined the institution of kingship. Modern scholars increasingly sense that the final biblical author who shaped our present biblical text gave us a vibrant portrayal of a very human David, with virtues and vices, but gave us enough hints about his vices to realize that we should not place David on a golden pedestal. Scholars suspect that the final form of the David narratives may have been crafted to critique the entire institution of kingship. We have been reading these texts for years, unwittingly being programmed to see the human and fallible nature of kings, while those in power have attempted for centuries to make people bow to the power of royalty by propagandizing their divine status with an appeal to these accounts. In reality, subversive biblical stories have been undercutting the propaganda of the ruling classes for years, at least for those who could read the Bible with eyes and minds wide open.

As we read the story of David, we discover that he, like Saul, incurred the wrath of a prophet for his actions. Again, we sense that even the high and mighty king was under the authority of the prophet. David incurred the wrath of Nathan when he acted with the unbridled power that so often typified the actions of men once given the authoritarian powers of kingship. After having seduced or raped Uriah's wife, Bathsheba (2 Sam 11:1-13), David had Uriah killed and took Bathsheba as his wife (2 Sam 11:14-26). Then the prophet entered with an antiroyal parable (2 Sam 12:1-15), which symbolized David as the rapacious herdsman who stole the poor man's single sheep and butchered it for a meal. Unlike most of the kings who would follow him, David repented, and thus affirmed the ideology of the biblical authors concerning the religious authority of the prophet over the king. David was subsequently seen as superior to many of the other kings, because he could humble himself before God, and the prophet!

There are some commentators who suspect that perhaps Bathsheba may have seduced David by luring him to invite her to his palace. That may be true. But David is still guilty of rape, for he was a person in position of supreme power, and having sex with anyone (who was not his wife) was an act of supreme power over that individual. Politicians in Washington DC today should take notice of such an observation. When you are powerful, having sex with someone illicitly is an act of supreme sexual power and manipulation. Men of power in Washington DC may have women drawn to them because of who they are, but that does not absolve them. We can argue forever whether a politician seduced a woman or whether she seduced him. People in positions of power are ultimately the ones who are responsible, and sexual liaisons are their betrayal of the public trust. Sometimes political leaders are handsome and charming and that acts as a sexual magnet, but they need to be even more moral in their behavior than others, for such sexual activity or even a hint of sexual activity can result in a great loss of public trust, which damages the function of government, as was the case with President Clinton in the 1990s.

Even more disturbing is when politicians who spout rhetoric about family values in congress are guilty of sexual liaisons outside of marriage, as was the case recently with one of our local congressmen here in Louisiana, David Vitter, who consorted with prostitutes in Washington early in his career. When this was discovered years later, his response to his voting electorate was that he had made his peace with God, and his sexual life was none of their business. Wrong! The politician may make his peace with God, but he also has to make his peace with us. In the Christian tradition there is absolution for the repentance of sins, but there also needs to be some form of penance on the human or social level. Amends have to be made in order to mitigate the results of the evil that has been done. There must be some form of justice. This is true for common folk; it is even truer for powerful politicians in the public view. Sex and power go together, it seems, and the prophetic words of judgment need to be forthcoming. Too often politicians (and preachers and television evangelists) seem to think that if they tell their constituency they are sorry for their sexual misconduct, they have done enough and they can continue with business as usual. Sadly their supporters accept this nonsense.

Ultimately, it is testimony to the power of the biblical text and the courage of the biblical authors that the story of David and Bathsheba could be told. The adultery of the king, and even more, the humiliation of the king before a prophet, was a story that one could not find elsewhere in the ancient world. This was truly an antiroyal narrative, for it proclaimed not only the weakness of a man who was king but his humbling before the prophet and God. Such a story punched holes through any propagandistic veil designed to portray the king as the representative of the gods to lowly people.

Though the memory of the Bathsheba incident was the most apparent indictment of David in the biblical text, a close reading of the promises to David in 2 Samuel 7 reveal yet another subtle critique of royal pride. Donald Murray skillfully demonstrates how this passage was a divine put-down of royal pride and pretensions. In 2 Samuel 4–6 David accomplished the unification of all Israel by the defeat of his enemies: Israelite, Jebusite, and Philistine. Especially after seizing Jerusalem and moving the ark of the covenant there, David proposed to build a temple to the

Lord. In so doing, he was imitating the behavior of Assyrian and Babylonian kings who often built temples to their patron deities after military victories and then placed inscriptions on those temples lauding their own military prowess, their rule over all of the nations around them, and their special status before the deity. We have numerous stereotypical reports of these endeavors. In those inscriptions, the ancient Near Eastern kings inquired of their professional court divinators whether they should proceed with the temple building, and after receiving the usual affirmative response, the kings would break ground. Sargon of Assyria built an entire city, Dur-Sharrukin, around 710 B.C.E. with inscriptions proclaiming this ideological rhetoric. David initially inquired of Nathan as to whether he should build a temple, and Nathan said yes. But quickly the Lord came to Nathan in a dream by night and sternly said to put on the brakes for the building plans, thus subverting the classic ancient Near Eastern royal ideology and David's attempted prideful actions.

The blessing of a future dynasty for David in 2 Samuel 7 was God's way of saying that the security of future descendants to sit upon the throne of Judah came from God alone and not the great military genius of David, founder and father of that future dynasty. The allusion to David as shepherd of the people was sarcasm apparently, for when the Mesopotamian kings spoke of their building projects, they called themselves shepherds.[9] This oracle to David was a blessing, to be sure, but also a slap in the face for David. Just when we thought the Bible was being nice to a king's reputation, a closer reading reveals otherwise.

The rebellion against David by his beloved son Absalom was yet another indictment of David. How weak is a king that he must endure such a rebellion. But the biblical narrative told the story in depth. David was unable to control any of his sons. The great king was powerful in the realm, but powerless in his family. The heir apparent to the throne, Amnon, raped his half-sister Tamar (2 Sam 13:1-22) and David did nothing. So Tamar's full brother, Absalom, the next heir apparent to the throne, killed Amnon (2 Sam 13:23-37) and fled the kingdom. Absalom was able to return from exile due to the efforts of General Joab (2 Sam 14:1-33), but then rose unsuccessfully in rebellion against his father (2 Sam 15:1–19:43). What a tragedy, and what testimony to the weakness of the great king, that his own beloved son rose against him and died. Would any other culture tell such a story about its king?

During the flight from Jerusalem, after Absalom seized the city, David was cursed by Shimei (2 Sam 16:10). He forbade his men to kill Shimei, for he knew that he deserved such scorn. His sons engaged in rape and violence, for they were like him. He raped Bathsheba and killed Uriah.[10] The biblical author recalled that small detail so that we might realize how judgment has fallen upon David in deserved fashion.

We are struck by how often people conveniently died and cleared the way for David's ascent to the throne. How cooperative of them! Critical scholars suspect that the biblical author invites us to actually be suspicious of David. In 1 Sam 25:2-42 Nabal opposed David, but died when his heart turned to "stone." David subsequently received Nabal's wealth and his wife, Abigail, as his own wife. Did Abigail perhaps poison Nabal after coming to David in humble fashion. Later 2 Sam 3:6-39 told of how Joab, David's kinsman and trusted general, killed Abner, a general who opposed David but was willing to negotiate a truce with David. David mourned Abner's death and Joab's treachery during the truce, but Joab remained in command. An Amalekite came to David seeking reward for his claim to have killed Saul according to 2 Sam 1:1-16. David had him executed. But why did he think David would reward him for his news? Ishbaal (Ishbosheth), the surviving son of Saul, was killed according to 2 Sam 4:1-12, and his assassins came to David seeking their reward. David executed them. But why did these people come to David in the first place? The biblical author, I believe, invites us to suspect that covertly David supported these assassinations. Do we remember how John Poindexter and Oliver North gave President Ronald Reagan "absolute deniability" in the Iran-Contra scandal in the 1980s by claiming that the president knew nothing of what he and others in the president's staff were doing? Since when does a president not know what his staff is doing on such an important international issue? Are we, the American public, that stupid? Likewise, David sought to have "absolute deniability" in his own age, but the biblical author invites us to be suspicious.

In an appendix to the book of 2 Samuel we discover the story of how David undertook a census of Israel (2 Samuel 24). Some opposed this census (2 Sam 24:4), perhaps because they suspected it was the prelude to military conscription (the biblical author did not say one way or the other). In 2 Sam 24:9 Joab reported the results of the census by enumerating those who could "draw the sword." It sounds like military conscription. For this act of arrogance David was punished by God. Again, we must ask, what nation in the ancient world would tell such a story, when it was naturally assumed that creating armies was the normal activity of kings?

This story shared a common theme with the Bathsheba narrative. In both accounts David strove to exercise the power and authority that kings so often have: he sought to have his way in matters of sexual prowess and military accomplishments. He failed in both. It seems that the biblical author was intent upon demonstrating that when David sought power or women, he brought trouble upon the nation—he brought a "series of disasters in both political and private spheres."[11] Seen in this light the biblical accounts appear to provide a warning for kings of any age to beware of those royal desires that afflict people in power. To indulge in the satisfaction of one's lust for power and women will bring your downfall or at least the dishonoring of your legacy. It is advice that might best be heeded by congressmen in Washington. Come to think of it, this is advice that should be heeded by clergy, many of whom have brought about their own downfall by financial or sexual escapades (or both). In New Orleans and Baton Rouge in the past generation we have seen the downfall of two famous local television evangelists because of their weakness for women, one who was the nationally famous Jimmy Swaggart (both belonged to the same denomination, the Assemblies of God). Those who are in power too often believe that they will not be caught. Our biblical author has recalled the sins of David for us as a warning. It is too bad that those who quote the Bible too often do not read or heed its message.

The mere fact that the Bible is willing to tell us a story about the impotence of a king is a powerful statement against the institution of kingship. We might not notice this at first reading, but we have been brainwashed by the Bible to view kings as human. Prior to the Bible, and outside the biblical text, kings were perceived as gods or at least semi-divine. To portray a king as sexually impotent is to undermine the basic ancient understanding of kingship. David was impotent. Great and mighty David was impotent. As an old man he was incapable of having sex. We can read it in 1 Kings 1:1-4:

> [1]King David was old and advanced in years; and although they covered him with clothes, he could not get warm. [2]So his servants said to him, "Let a young virgin be sought for my lord the king, and let her wait on the king, and be his attendant; let her lie in your bosom, so that my lord the king may be warm." [3]So they searched for a beautiful girl throughout all the territory of Israel, and found Abishag, the Shunammite, and brought her to the king. [4]The girl was very beautiful. She became the king's attendant and served him, but the king did not know her sexually.

David, who had sex with so many women, could not make love to a beautiful woman in bed with him. Did the servants find this young girl in order to reveal to those in positions of authority in Jerusalem that the old king was dying? Perhaps, they did. Perhaps, this led Adonijah to move forward and have himself crowned king. Royal sexual potency was a powerful and dramatic symbol to ancient peoples. Generally kings in the ancient world (and in movies about olden times) were heroically described as manly and virile up to the time of their death. In the ancient Near East kings symbolically brought fertility to the land and to people by virtue of their sexual virility, and, to that end, kings in Mesopotamia engaged in a sexual union with the high priestess during the New Year festival of *Akitu* in order to ensure that the crops would be bountiful in the coming year. The Mesopotamian king represented the fertility god Dumuzi or Tammuz and the high priestess represented the goddess Inanna or Ishtar.[12] To acknowledge that the king was sexually impotent would imply to many superstitious folk that the crops of the land might not grow in the coming year. To admit that a king was impotent is to declare he is no longer worthy to be king.

To admit sexual impotence on David's part was a major admission. In fact, since he was the founder of the Davidic dynasty of kings, which ruled for over three hundred years, this attribution of impotence to David actually implied that symbolically this was true of all his later heirs in some way. Thus, all the kings of Judah were descended from an impotent old man. To the popular mind this was a way of saying the dynasty truly failed the nation. 1 Kgs 1:1-4 was a very nasty political text. The mere fact that it began the book of Kings implies that it set the stage for the nature of the narratives that follow. The biblical books of 1 and 2 Kings tell us all about impotent kings.[13]

Louis XIV, the Great Sun King, ruled France with power and lived in splendor. Here in New Orleans years ago we had a museum display of beautiful artwork and other items from his palace to celebrate the era of French imperial glory that gave rise to colonial expansion into America, including the founding of our own city. The display, however, did not recall that he became an old and feeble king, still retaining the awesome power of the throne, which, in turn, led others to manipulate him. Louis' favorite son, the Duc du Maine, sired by Louis with an already-married woman, and Mme. De Maintenon, a woman privately married to Louis, manipulated Louis and convinced him to disown the Duc d'Orleans, Louis' nephew and the regent, and in his place to make the Duc du Maine the successor to the throne. It was Adonijah and Solomon once more. Such is the way of powerful kings; sometimes they are totally power-less.[14] Sometimes kings are pawns to the people they thought were their own pawns.

Furthermore, in 1 Kgs 2:1-9 David gave final instructions to Solomon before he died. In these instructions he told Solomon to kill Joab, the general who served David well but at times in high-handed fashion (as when he killed Absalom), and Shimei, the person who cursed David but supposedly was forgiven by him. Commentators point out that these last words of David make him appear vindictive and do not leave a good impression of either David or Solomon. They foreshadowed the vindictive politics that would typify much of the ruling David dynasts throughout the next three centuries.[15]

IV

The Deuteronomistic History continued with more stories about kings and the prophets who criticized them. Solomon was the next target of critique by the biblical historians. Was not Solomon praised for being rich and wise? Yes, he was. But if we read carefully the narrative in 1 Kings 1–11, we can see the dark side of Solomon and the inherent evil of kings surface in his person and his actions. Commentators have assumed for years that when the prophet Samuel spoke his words of warning in 1 Samuel 8 about kings in general, he was talking about the rule of Solomon in particular and all other kings who imitated Solomon.

When we read the narrative in 1 Kings 1–11 we discover many negative statements about Solomon lurking between the lines.[16] (1) Solomon became king instead of the expected heir, Adonijah, because of the machinations of his mother Bathsheba and the prophet Nathan. While Adonijah was being crowned king, these two convinced an old and feeble David that Solomon had been promised the throne. There was no account of such a promise. If there were such a promise, the biblical author surely would have recorded it. Its absence invites suspicion. Bathsheba and Nathan had a counter coronation ceremony with David present, so that Adonijah and his supporters were intimidated and relinquished their claim to make Adonijah king (1 Kgs 1:5-53). Essentially, Solomon's rise to power was illegitimate and the biblical text gives us enough hints to figure that out.

(2) Solomon began his reign with a bloodbath according to 1 Kings 1. He killed Adonijah, Joab, Shimei (1 Kgs 2:13-46), and probably others for relatively lame excuses. Yes, David told Solomon to do this. That is, of course, unless our biblical author wished us to read between the lines and notice that only Solomon heard the words of David, and we realize

that David previously was so feeble as perhaps to be unable to convey such a complex message. Regardless of whether David gave this advice, the biblical text began the story of Solomon's reign by describing the bloodbath by which he came to power. We view the "malicious and self-destructive side to Israel's great monarch,"[17] and this was quite the introduction by the biblical author, who thus subliminally paints a negative portrait for us before we even begin to read of Solomon's royal accomplishments.

(3) Solomon was a typical king who practiced power politics. He married Pharaoh's daughter (1 Kgs 3:1) and daughters of other rulers, probably as a result of trade and political alliances. He allowed these women to bring the worship of their gods into Jerusalem and the surrounding areas, and he built shrines for their gods (1 Kgs 11:1-13). His one thousand wives were a reflection of his power (not sexual appetite) for they came with alliances with other nations. But his marriages symbolized his overweening power. To recall such marriages also implied that most likely there was corruption and double-dealing that occurred in the palace continually. "The size of the royal harem signals corruption rather than prosperity or splendor,"[18] for they signified the court intrigue that can destroy integrity and compromise the morality of the ruler.

(4) He instituted corveé, the practice of forcing people to work on the royal building projects (1 Kgs 5:13-18; 9:15; 12:4). This would remind Israelites of any age of the onerous labor imposed on the Israelite slaves in Egypt. Solomon became pharaoh to his own people. It appears, however, that Solomon exempted his own tribe of Judah from this onerous burden.[19]

(5) Though Solomon was praised for building the temple in Jerusalem, he actually put more effort into his own palace. The temple was constructed in seven years (1 Kgs 6:38) while his palace required thirteen years (1 Kgs 7:1).

(6) Though Deut 17:16 said that kings should not have horses, Solomon had 12,000 horses and horsemen, plus 1,400 chariots, a sign of tremendous military power (1 Kgs 4:26; 10:26-29).

(7) In scandalous fashion Solomon gave away some of the land of Israel, which should never have been done. He gave twenty cities in Galilee to Hiram, king of Tyre (1 Kgs 9:10-14).

(8) Solomon refortified old Canaanite centers of power, Megiddo, Hazor, and Gezer (1 Kgs 9:15-19), which does not seem significant unless you realize that these cities are deep within Israel. Solomon was fortifying these cities not against foreign invasion, but against his own people.

He was a dictator whose regime needed to be propped up by military force.

(9) He created twelve administrative districts for the country (1 Kgs 4:7-19), which differed from the old tribal borders. Apparently he was trying to replace tribal structures with a new governmental system, which insulted traditional old values of the people.

(10) Most significantly, there was no reference to Solomon seeking the advice of a prophet in all of these activities. Given the nature of the accounts elsewhere in the Deuteronomistic History, this was a conspicuous detail to be missing. Solomon did all these things of his own accord; they did not come from God. Hence, 1 Kgs 11:6 simply said that Solomon did evil, and in the larger message (perhaps a dream theophany) given by God to Solomon in 1 Kgs 11:9-13, God told Solomon that his sinfulness would lead to the collapse of his kingdom after his death.

Solomon led a conspicuously consumptive lifestyle, and the biblical authors made this quite evident. We read in 1 Kgs 4:22-23, 26-27:

> [22]Solomon's provision for one day was thirty cors of choice flour, and sixty cors of meal, [23]ten fat oxen, and twenty pasture-fed cattle, one hundred sheep, besides deer, gazelles, roebucks, and fatted fowl. . . . [26]Solomon also had forty thousand stalls of horses for his chariots, and twelve thousand horsemen. [27]Those officials supplied provisions for King Solomon and for all who came to King Solomon's table, each one in his month; they let nothing be lacking.

Under Solomon, "economics of privilege" replaced any concern for equitable distribution of resources to the general citizenry, or at least this is the impression that the biblical author left for us.[20]

All of these details were remembered by the Deuteronomistic Historian. In between the words of praise for Solomon's wisdom and wealth and his construction of the temple, there were hints given by the biblical author that Solomon was a tyrant. Since Solomon became the image for the archetypal king, we perceive the biblical author's view of kingship even in the midst of praising one of its most famous kings.

V

The stories of Saul, David, and Solomon have been popular Sunday school stories and have inspired many movies and television shows. A quick reading may present these men as heroes, perhaps with the human vices and mistakes that makes them all the more dramatic and heroic for us. But if we read the texts very closely and observe the subtle additions, comments, and even sequencing of stories that have been provided by the Deuteronomistic Historian, we notice a more negative assessment. Kings and their actions are seen negatively. Kings were to be subordinate to the Word of the Lord as it was proclaimed through the prophets. Essentially Saul, David, and Solomon fell short in many ways. Granted, David inspired the image of the future messiah. But that messiah will be greater than him. The Deuteronomistic Historians have cleverly taken traditions that were positive about kings and kingship, but, by adding their own theological editorial observations, they provided a very powerful critique unlike anything we might discover in the contemporary world of Israel, or even up through the early modern period. We have before us a message truly worth heeding.

8. Deuteronomistic History III: The Divided Monarchies

I

The story of the kings continued in the rest of the two books of Kings: again and again kings sinned and prophets admonished them. Eventually the two nations of Israel and Judah fell before foreign conquerors because God punished both nations for their sins, especially the sins of their kings.

Rehoboam lost the kingdom that his grandfather, David, created and his father, Solomon, stewarded. When Solomon died, Rehoboam went to Shechem to meet with the elders of Israel. An exile from Egypt, Jeroboam, who fled from Solomon, returned to speak for the people and to ask that Rehoboam make their tax and work burden lighter than it had been under him (1 Kgs 12:1-5). Rehoboam spoke with the old counselors who advised Solomon to lighten the burden, but when he spoke with the young men who had grown up with him (probably his half-brothers from Solomon's many wives), they encouraged him to get tough with the people, a policy followed by many world rulers and national business leaders today (1 Kgs 12:6-11). They advised him to say the following (vv. 10-11):

> [10]My little finger is thicker than my father's loins. [11]Now, whereas my father laid on you a heavy yoke, I will add to your yoke. My father disciplined you with whips, but I will discipline you with scorpions.

There are two nasty statements here. He should say that his little finger was thicker than his father's thigh, which is the largest muscle on the human body. But there may be a double entendre. "Little finger" may refer to the penis, in which case, he would coarsely say that his sexual organ was larger than his father's "thigh," which can also mean loins or sexual organ. He would imply that he will treat them more roughly than Solomon did. He should also say that he will use scorpions rather than the whips his father used. "Scorpions" were whips that had small metal balls attached at the end so that when a person was flailed with a scorpion, his flesh was ripped off. Whips were used to encourage slaves; scorpions were used on prisoners of war, because eventually the whipping killed them.

When Rehoboam went before the crowd, he uttered the second saying, but not the first (1 Kgs 12:12-19). Of course, when the people heard this, they yelled, "To your tents, O Israel" (1 Kgs 12:16), an expression calling for military mobilization. It was a declaration of war, a declaration of independence from Davidic rule. Rehoboam was stupid and totally out of touch with his people, and he precipitated a rebellion by his arrogant actions. How many politicians are out of touch with people today? Rehoboam was the typical king of the age. Raised in the pampered luxury of the Jerusalem palace, born with the sense that he had a right to rule, overwhelmed with his own sense of privilege, he lost the kingdom in an act of arrogance and braggadocio. The northern tribes went away from Shechem and made Jeroboam their king (1 Kgs 12:20).

Ahijah of Shiloh in 1 Kgs 14:7-16 uttered a severe judgment oracle to the wife of Jeroboam, declaring that Jeroboam's child, Abijah, would die when his mother returned to the city of Tirzah and that Jeroboam's dynasty would be brought to a bloody end. Jeroboam was succeeded by his son, Nadab, but Nadab and the entire family of Jeroboam was killed by Baasha, who became king of Israel (1 Kgs 15:25-30). In general, the historian recalled Jeroboam negatively because he built the golden calves in Dan and Bethel (1 Kgs 12:25-33), one in each city. His purpose was to make those two cities the sites for pilgrims, so that the pilgrims would not go down to Jerusalem and be influenced by propaganda that declared a Davidide should be king over all of Israel and not Jeroboam. He presented the calves to the people by saying, "Here are your gods, O Israel, who brought you up out of the land of Egypt" (1 Kgs 12:28). The word for "gods" might be translated in the singular as "god," in which case the reference would be to Yahweh, who brought Israelites forth in the exodus. Both polytheists and Yahweh devotees could have been happy with that vague expression. Jeroboam also might have implied that the "god" was invisibly enthroned above the calf. If this was the case, his actions would not sound so much like idolatry, for Yahweh could not be seen and the calf was merely a pedestal. However, if he implied that "god" or the "gods" were in the calf, then it would sound more like traditional Canaanite religion wherein the calf or bull can be a symbol for the presence of a powerful fertility deity such as El or Baal.

At this time in history Israelites were inherently polytheists, worshiping Yahweh, Baal, El, and probably other gods. I believe Jeroboam's words were meant to be ambiguous, so that they appealed to Yahweh devotees, who sensed Yahweh was above the calf invisibly enthroned, and also to El or Baal devotees, who saw their patron deity in the calf image.[1] The Deuteronomistic Historians interpreted his actions as supporting polytheistic worship. Perhaps, Jeroboam thought he was being clever, and perhaps he thought his was a traditional form of Yahwistic piety, but his calves permitted the worship of gods, El and Baal, who rivaled Yahweh according to later monotheistic authors. Such is the way that kings and politicians work—they try to be clever and please everyone in the short run and instead cause long-term damage.

Jeroboam I was confronted also by a "man of God" while standing by the altar in Bethel (1 Kgs 13:1-10). The "man of God" cursed the altar, caused Jeroboam's hand to wither, and then cured the hand (a rather generous act under the circumstances). The narrative reminds us of the confrontation of Amaziah the priest by Amos (Amos 7:10-17) some 170 years later,[2] although the story in 1 Kings 13 may have been influenced by the Amos account when the Deuteronomistic History was generated in the late seventh century B.C.E. The image of a prophet storming into the royal sanctuary and confronting the king during ritual, which was an activity that legitimated the personal authority of the king, bespoke courage and assumed the authority of the prophet over the king.

In 1 Kgs 16:1-4 we have a short account of how the prophet, Jehu ben Hanani, spoke a word of judgment against King Baasha of Israel, who had killed all the family of Jeroboam and became king instead. Jehu declared that his family would be destroyed like Jeroboam's, and indeed, Baasha's son, Elah, was killed by Zimri, and Zimri then destroyed the entire family of Baasha.

1 Kgs 20:1-43 recorded in detail an unusual story in which King Ahab defeated Ben-hadad of Aram (Syria) in war. Although initially Ben-hadad threatened Ahab with defeat (vv. 1-6), a nameless prophet declared that Ahab would prevail in battle (vv. 13-14). Ahab attacked Ben-hadad with trickery while the latter was drunk and Ahab sent the Aramean troops scurrying. When Ben-hadad attacked again at a later time (vv. 23-30), he

was defeated once more and Ahab took Ben-hadad alive. Instead of killing Ben-hadad, as he should have, Ahab made a political and economic treaty with him in order to make money through trade in the Aramean city of Damascus (vv. 31-34). Then an unnamed prophet spoke a dramatic oracle against King Ahab because he had captured King Ben-hadad and decided not to kill him (vv. 35-43). The prophet declared that Ahab ought to die for this, for the Lord had set Ben-hadad aside for destruction, and now Ahab would have to die instead. Indeed, later Ahab died in battle fighting those very same Arameans (1 Kgs 22:29-38). The two narratives testified to the greed of King Ahab, as well as his political folly. Instead of executing Ben-hadad and weakening Aram, Ahab cut a deal in order to get money. Eventually he died in battle fighting those same Arameans from whom he thought he could make a fortune. Such is the folly of kings. Ahab sacrificed the lives of his soldiers to win battles and then he frittered away the success of such victories with his political machinations.

As an interlude in the accounts of King Ahab's wars we hear the tale of Naboth's vineyard. 1 Kgs 21:1-16 recounted how King Ahab and Queen Jezebel cheated Naboth out of his vineyard and had him executed. 1 Kgs 21:17-29 reported how Elijah then condemned Ahab and thus functioned as the advocate for the rights of Israelite landowners against the rapaciousness of kings.[3] The prophet, not the king, appeared as the defender of the individual property rights. As we read the account, we discover humor and sarcasm. When Ahab sought to buy the vineyard, Naboth told the king he could not sell the land that belonged to his family for years, for it was customary that land remained with the family and could not be sold by an individual. The mere fact that the Bible recorded how a simple citizen defied the great king is rather amazing. After Naboth declined to sell his vineyard, the great and mighty king went to his room and pouted. Verse 4 said, "He lay down on his bed, turned away his face, and would not eat." What a spoiled child! Fortunately for him his wife Jezebel acted like his mommy and came in to find out the problem. Once she learned of the vineyard, she sprang into action and unleashed her devious plan to have Naboth executed. She wrote letters in Ahab's name, used his seal, sent the letters to powerful people in the city, and found two liars to accuse Naboth of blasphemy, which ultimately led to his death by stoning. She then went to Ahab and informed him that the vineyard was his. Wait a minute—who was the real king here? Was it Jezebel? Ahab appeared not even to know what was going on, and then at the end of the affair he silently went like an oaf and got his vineyard, apparently without asking any questions. The king was responsible for justice, but he did not inquire whether any injustice had occurred. The king lived in the shadow of his wife—who was both a foreigner and a priestess for the Phoenician god Baal. Ahab appeared in the story as a weak and incompetent king who took orders from his wife. For the ancient Israelite audience this was great humor—still is today, I suppose.

Elijah condemned Ahab, for, after all, he was king and had to take responsibility for what happened. Our biblical authors arranged the sequence of the narratives in such a way that this account was followed by the chapter in which Ahab's death was told—fitting justice for the incompetent and evil king. Scholarly commentators point out that the biblical author recounted the story of the vineyard seizure almost like a parable, and its narrative outline seems to have been influenced by the account of David's murder of Uriah and seizure of Bathsheba. As a parable it condemned kings and affirmed the rights of common citizens over against the king in economic matters.[4]

The story of the vineyard and Elijah's judgment on Ahab was followed by the account of Ahab's death in battle, giving us the impression that the dramatic judgment of God came down upon Ahab. How impressive that the Bible would tell us in straightforward fashion of how Ahab died in battle in 1 Kings 22. Ahab disguised himself so as not to be recognized (v. 30), but an Aramean archer shot him by chance supposing him to be simply another officer on the field of battle (v. 34). How different this is from political reports of battle in the ancient world and our own day. In the thirteenth century B.C.E. the powerful pharaoh of Egypt, Ramses II, lost a battle against the Hittites at the Syrian site of Kadesh on the Orontes in 1286 B.C.E. Even though he held the battlefield, he lost half of his army. The Hittites withdrew because they achieved their goals and they had battles to fight elsewhere in their empire. Ramses II returned to Egypt and began a propaganda campaign to declare the battle a victory—one that he won single-handed after his troops had failed him. How many rulers and dictators in our modern era claim victory in the face of defeat. I am reminded of Iraqi claims of victory as their armies retreated in the Second Gulf War. I am painfully reminded of the inflated casualty figures of the enemy reported on nightly news to the American public during the Vietnam War. In contrast, the biblical text had no problem recalling ignominious defeats of their kings.

Some Old Testament historians suggest that the king in the story originally was not Ahab but a king of Israel who lived years later, perhaps

Joram, son of Ahab, who was reported to have been wounded in battle against the Syrians (2 Kgs 9:14-26), or even more likely Jehoahaz many years later. The biblical authors placed Ahab's name in the story for dramatic effect as they proclaimed that the kings ought to have listened to the prophets, and that powerful kings, like Ahab, who stole Naboth's vineyard and murdered Naboth, deserved the punishment that the Lord sent.[5] Whether the king was Ahab or some other king from a later generation is irrelevant, for in its final form, the biblical narrative testified to the petty machinations of kings who waste their people's lives and their nation's resources in order to make profit for themselves and their rich friends and thus bring ruin upon their countries. One cannot help but think of so many poor African countries, like Zimbabwe, whose leaders make fortunes by twisting the national economy, while the poor peasants starve to death. Or again, have our own leaders led us into wars in the Middle East simply to preserve oil interests that profit the investors in oil companies?

II

A subtle mode of criticizing the institution of kingship was provided by the editorial work of the Deuteronomistic Historians in the traditions about Elijah and Elisha. They selectively chose some narrative accounts from the oral tradition for specific theological and political reasons. Within the Elijah and Elisha narratives one senses a pattern wherein kings failed to do those things for which they were most responsible, then prophets accomplished these tasks instead. The role of kings in any society was to guarantee security for people and to protect their property. In the ancient world the king was responsible for fertility by interceding with the divine realm to bring good crop yields. This was an integral part of royal ceremonies, such as the *Sed* festival in Egypt, which renewed kingship and the fertility of the land, and the *Akitu* New Year's ceremony in Mesopotamia, which brought protection to the land from flooding and chaos, as well as ensuring fertility of the land. Our editor of the books of Kings placed prophetic stories into the greater narrative that reflected how kings failed to protect property and provide food while the prophets fulfilled these functions.[6]

At the beginning of the Elijah narratives, we learn that a drought and a famine have struck the land of Israel, and this drought was announced to the king by the word of the prophet (1 Kgs 17:1). The king was helpless to end the drought until finally the word of the Lord came through the prophet once more (1 Kgs 18:41-46).

Elijah or Elisha provided food on several occasions. In 1 Kgs 17:8-16 Elijah resided with a widow of Zarephath, who was a foreigner, and he ensured that her jar of meal and jug of oil did not become empty during the famine. In similar fashion, Elisha helped a widow by preventing a creditor from seizing her land by multiplying oil in jars so that she could pay her debt (2 Kgs 4:1-7). Whereas the king failed to provide food during a drought and later failed to protect a widow's land, a prophet intervened to bring a boundless supply of food in both instances. In both Mesopotamia and Egypt, kings bragged about how they protected poor widows. Elijah and Elisha both usurped the function of the king because Israel's kings were remiss in this honorable task.

During a famine caused by a siege of Samaria (2 Kgs 6:24-30) the king again failed to provide food for his people. When called upon by a woman for help (we do not know if she was a widow), he said, "How can I help you?" (v. 27). She remonstrated that she had made a deal with another woman that both would kill and eat their small children. The woman who complained had given her child to be eaten, but the other woman had reneged on her promise, so the first woman appealed to the king to force the other woman to surrender her child. The king was appalled by the nature of these actions, but the deeper implication was that the king, the perceived source of fertility, failed completely in his royal function. It is incredible that the biblical narratives included such a heart-rending account in such blunt fashion to so humiliate the king.[7] In contrast to the helpless king, however, stood the prophet, ready to bring fertility and food to the people. In other narratives Elisha provided food for one hundred people by multiplying twenty loaves of barley and fresh ears of grain brought by a man from Baal-shalishah (2 Kgs 4:42-44), foreshadowing Jesus feeding the masses with a few loaves and fish. Not only did the prophet provide food, the prophet elevated the quality of food to be consumed. In 2 Kgs 4:38-41 Elisha made unfit stew edible. (I know some restaurants that could sorely use the skills of this prophet.) We can sense a bit of sarcasm by the biblical editors as they inserted these stories into our text to comment on royal incompetence.

The king was seen as the source of life. But it was Elijah who raised the widow of Zarephath's son (1 Kgs 17:17-24) and Elisha who raised the Shunammite woman's son (2 Kgs 4:8-37). Again, we observe paired stories about both Elijah and Elisha in these crucial activities. Raising someone from the dead was a dramatic action, for in the ancient world this was the prerogative of the gods, and perhaps some would attribute this power of resuscitation only to a fertility god who brought the world back to life in the spring. Since the patron god associated with the king in the accounts of Elijah and Elisha was the god of vegetation and fertility, Baal, it appears that Elijah and Elisha usurped the authority of the fertility god sponsored by the royal cult. Apparently the king could not even choose the correct deity.

This poor choice of deity by the king was most evident in the contest on Mount Carmel where Elijah defeated the prophets of Baal in a contest to bring fire down from the heavens to ignite a sacrifice (1 Kgs 18:20-40). The story was about the defeat of the god Baal by Yahweh, and although Baal was the god of fertility, he was shown to be powerless. After the contest the drought ended (1 Kgs 18:41-46), which added insult to injury upon Baal's inability to provide fertility and food. Behind the story, of course, was the implication that Ahab, the king, chose the wrong deity for fertility, another stunning critique of the king and his devoted supporters.

In the ancient world the king as the source of life was responsible for providing water through irrigation, as in Egypt and Mesopotamia. The king should have had at his disposal divinators who could inform when the famine would begin or end, but instead he had to heed the prophetic word. Elijah predicted for Ahab that there would be a drought (1 Kgs 17:1-7) and when the drought would end (1 Kgs 18:41-46). The prophet brought water, while the king waited for the word of the prophet to discern what was happening.

We have other accounts that spoke of the direct authority of the prophet over the king. The most dramatic scene was the appearance of Elijah before Ahab to condemn him for seizing Naboth's vineyard and executing him (1 Kgs 21:1-24). The prophetic judgment reads as follows (1 Kgs 21:20-24),

> [20]Ahab said to Elijah, "Have you found me, O my enemy?" He answered, "I have found you. Because you have sold yourself to do what is evil in the sight of the LORD, [21]I will bring disaster on you; I will consume you, and will cut off from Ahab every male, bond or free, in Israel; [22]and I will make your house like the house of Jeroboam son of Nebat, and like the house of Baasha son of Ahijah, because you have provoked me to anger and have caused Israel to sin. [23]Also concerning Jezebel the LORD said, 'The dogs shall eat Jezebel within the bounds of Jezreel.' [24]Anyone belonging to Ahab who dies in the city the dogs shall eat; and anyone of his who dies in the open country the birds of the air shall eat."

After Ahab was killed in battle, his body was brought back to Samaria, his chariot was washed at the pool of Samaria, dogs licked up his blood, and prostitutes bathed in the pool containing some of that blood (1 Kgs 22:38). Ahab repented before Elijah, hence part of the judgment was withdrawn by God. Ahab did not live to see his family destroyed, but his son Joram, king of Israel, and old Queen Jezebel, Ahab's wife, would be killed by general Jehu in the next generation (2 Kgs 9:14-37).

This narrative portrayed Elijah the prophet standing in judgment over the king and as a spokesperson for the economic value system of pastoral Israel over against some form of mercantilism, apparently advocated with the presence of the Phoenician political representatives in Israel.[8] This image of a prophet condemning a king for economic injustice indicates that Israel took justice for the poor more seriously than did other peoples.[9]

In 1 Kings 22 we have the story of how Micaiah ben Imlah opposed the will of King Ahab of Israel and King Jehoshaphat of Judah to go forth to war against the king of Syria. In this narrative the king had his own royal court prophets, four hundred in number, who gave him support by declaring that he would be victorious in battle. King Jehoshaphat suggested that they hear the opinion of another prophet, and so Micaiah ben Imlah was brought forth by King Ahab. But Micaiah was sullen and gave a halfhearted encouragement to go forth to fight. When forced to speak honestly, he spoke of ill results for the king, including the death of the king of Israel, Ahab. In 1 Kgs 22:17-23 we read:

> [17]Then Micaiah said, "I saw all Israel scattered on the mountains, like sheep that have no shepherd; and the Lord said, 'These have no master; let each one go home in peace.'" [18]The king of Israel said to Jehoshaphat, "Did I not tell you that he would not prophesy anything favorable about me, but only disaster?"
>
> [19]Then Micaiah said, "Therefore hear the word of the Lord: I saw the Lord sitting on his throne, with all the host of heaven standing beside him to the right and to the left of him. [20]And the Lord said, 'Who will entice Ahab, so that he may go up and fall at Ramoth-gilead?' Then one said one thing, and another said another, [21]until a spirit came forward and stood before the Lord, saying, 'I will entice him.' [22]'How?' the Lord asked him. He replied, 'I will go out and be a lying spirit in the mouth of all his prophets.' Then the Lord said, 'You are to entice him, and you shall succeed; go out and do it.' [23]So you see, the Lord has put a lying spirit in the mouth of all these your prophets; the Lord has decreed disaster for you."

Micaiah really knew how to gall King Ahab of Israel, as well as pretty rudely insulting his professional court prophets. Angered by Micaiah's response, Ahab had Micaiah imprisoned until his return. But the king never returned alive. As noted above, he died in battle, and his blood was licked by dogs (1 Kgs 22:29-38).

Micaiah ben Imlah in this account was extremely courageous, for he had the audacity to contradict four hundred court prophets of Ahab. How many critics of the government today would have the courage to go against the opinions of so many of their "professional" colleagues, as Micaiah did. Political advisors in the inner circles of power so often become trapped by "groupthink," the pressure to go along with the other advisors in the inner circles. Micaiah directly assaulted the king by insulting his professional court prophets, or political stooges.[10] Today we have political advisors who give political leaders the advice they want to hear so that they may go forth and do what they wanted to do all along. Such is the way of political stooges in our own age also.

A sweet and charming little story was the account of the Israelite maid who advised the Syrian general and her master, Naaman, to go to her homeland of Israel to be healed of his leprosy. Within this account was yet another nasty little barb taken at a nameless Israelite king, but from the context of the narrative in the greater plot of the book of 2 Kings, we would assume that it might be an Omride ruler. Naaman had his own king send a message to the king of Israel hoping that the king could act on behalf of his deity and heal Naaman of his leprosy (2 Kgs 5:5-6). Of course, the prerogative to heal belonged to the king and his royal divinators, according to the understanding of the ancient Near East, but according to the biblical text, the king of Israel condemned himself unwittingly (2 Kgs 5:7): "When the king of Israel read the letter, he tore his clothes and said, 'Am I God, to give death or life, that this sends word to me to cure a man of his leprosy.'" By his own words the king of Israel clearly admitted that he lacked the power to heal. Of course, Naaman then went to the prophet Elisha who sent Naaman to the Jordan River to be cured. Of the many messages found in the text, one is that the king by far is subordinate to the prophet in the art of healing.[11]

The final scenario in the conflict between the prophets and the royal house of the Omrides, of which Ahab was a member, was the narrative of the revolution inspired by the prophets. This story could easily have inspired people over the years to rebel against kings and tyrants. The story is told in detail in 2 Kings 9–10. Elisha sent a young prophet to the city of Ramoth-gilead to anoint Jehu, a general, as king over Israel and to commission him to kill all the members of the royal family (2 Kgs 9:1-13). Jehu then went forth and killed Joram, king of Israel, and Ahaziah, king of Judah, both descended from Omri, at the same time, after which he went to Jezreel and killed Jezebel, the wife of deceased King Ahab (2 Kgs 9:14-37). Thus, the key leaders in the Omride family were killed. Jehu continued the purge by killing seventy sons of Ahab in Samaria (2 Kgs 10:1-17) and then slaughtering the worshipers of Baal in their temple (2 Kgs 10:18-27). This was an incredible story for the biblical author to record. It testified to how a prophet, obviously directed by God, instigated a revolt that led to the death of two kings as well as their followers. The story was told in detail so that those who read the Bible cannot avoid reading this account and drawing the conclusion that tyrannical kings can be justly overthrown by those who adhere to the will of God.

This narrative was immediately followed by the story of yet another revolution. Athaliah, the wife of the slain Ahaziah, king of Judah, seized control in Judah after her husband's death and killed the rest of the royal family. One child, Joash, however, was hidden and protected (2 Kgs 11:1-3). Athaliah was also part of the Omride family. After six years, Jehoiada, a priest, led a rebellion against Athaliah and placed Joash on the throne as a seven-year-old king (2 Kgs 11:4-21). Thus, we have two stories in sequence about rebellions against rulers that are portrayed by the biblical authors as inspired by the prophets and priests of God. This is dangerous literature for people to read, for it might give them the idea to rebel against their own kings. In the eighteenth-century American countryside the most commonly owned book, and most frequently read book, was the Bible. Coincidence?

III

Later narratives in 2 Kings need not be discussed in great detail. Nevertheless, it is worth mentioning that the only two good kings in the estimation of the biblical author were Kings Hezekiah (2 Kings 18–20) and Josiah (2 Kings 22–23), both rulers in Judah. They were deemed to be good kings because they worshiped Yahweh rather exclusively, even though they probably were not monotheists by our definition. They also heeded the advice of prophets, and Josiah was shown the rediscovered Book of the Law and very seriously followed its directives (2 Kgs 22:3-20). But even when recalling the traditions about these two kings, the biblical author put forth a word of judgment against good King Hezekiah. In 2 Kgs 20:12-19 we are told that Hezekiah entertained envoys from the king of Babylon and showed them all the treasures in his storehouses (v. 13). In doing this, Hezekiah displayed "pride, arrogance, and complacency," which rather undercut the image that he was wholeheartedly devoted to Yahweh.[12] Subsequently Isaiah came to him and told him how foolish he was to do this, declaring that someday the Babylonians would come and despoil Judah of all its treasures because of his folly (vv. 14-18). Even the best kings can be dim-witted at times. The ultimate implication is that the truly faithful king is the ruler who submits to the will of God and the words of the prophets, and hence is not a tyrant.

IV

We have become so familiar with these accounts, we no longer see how radical their message is. The Deuteronomistic History proclaimed a message of faithfulness to one God, Yahweh, and obedience to the law, which among other things called for a fair and just society. In this highly interpreted theological history the biblical authors praised the notion of the ideal king, a king who would be faithful to Yahweh. What, of course, resulted from this interpretation of history was a portrayal of other kings as evil and the portrayal of the institution of kingship in general as evil. These narratives became sacred text for Jews and Christians. These texts sat in the Bible, like a ticking time bomb, waiting for someone to read them and draw the obvious implications that kings can be evil, kings can be overthrown, and that perhaps society can function best without kings. It was simply a matter of time before the Bible became widely printed and stories were read by the masses. Once that happened, the time bomb went off. The time bomb should still be going off today.

9. Primeval History

I

Biblical texts, which elevated average human beings to the level of kings and queens, criticized kingship, and a number of these texts may be found in what has been called the Primeval History of Genesis 1–11. We are tempted to suggest the exilic and postexilic periods as the point of origin for these accounts due to the presence of Mesopotamian themes in the literature. Genesis 1–11 exemplified dramatically the symbolic and theological mode by which biblical authors expressed themselves.

Most of the narratives in Genesis 2–11 are viewed by biblical scholars as a cycle of tales generated by an anonymous author called the Yahwist. (Past textbooks attributed the Yahwist tradition to the tenth-century B.C.E. court of Solomon, but now we attribute it to the sixth-century B.C.E. Babylonian Exile wherein it became the prologue to the preexisting Deuteronomistic History.) Supplemental narratives were added by exilic or postexilic Priestly editors to create our complete text in Genesis 1–11.[1] Yahwist stories included the creation of the Adam (generic man), the man and the woman in the garden, Cain and Abel, the flood, Noah and his sons, and the tower of Babel. The Priestly authors or editors included accounts of the cosmic creation (Gen 1:1–2:4a), the genealogy of Seth (Gen 5:1-32), portions of the flood narrative that envisioned the flood as a cosmic event (parts of Genesis 6–8), the covenant with Noah (Gen 9:1-15), and genealogies. Though most biblical theologians characterize the theology of Yahwist and Priestly texts separately, a few have argued that since the material eventually became a unity, it is best for us to stress the unity of the final text when doing biblical theology.[2]

II

World history textbooks often allude to John Ball as one of the key leaders in the famous English Peasants' Revolt of 1381, but too often the full story is not told. John Ball had been trained in Hebrew at Oxford University, so as he read the sacred text in the original tongue, he observed messages in the Bible that other preachers, theologians, and great leaders of the church did not see or ignored. In Genesis 1 he discerned that God had made "man" in his image and then made "man" into male and female, which implied for Ball that men and women were equal, for both were made equally in the image of God. What further impressed him was that this "image of God" elsewhere was attributed to kings. If the man and the woman were portrayed as royal personages in this biblical text and they were the ancestors of all humanity, perhaps that meant all people were equal and should have equal economic opportunity in a society in which there were no kings or nobility. For twenty years John Ball proclaimed his message in rural villages of northern England, and he eventually went to London to preach. A historian or chronicler of this age reported that he said the following:

> My good friends, things cannot go well in England, nor ever will until everything shall be in common; when there shall be neither vassal nor Lord and all distinctions leveled, when the lords shall be no more masters than ourselves. How ill have they used us? And for what reason do they thus hold us in bondage? Are we not all descended from the same parents, Adam and Eve? And what can they show or what reasons give, why they should be more masters than ourselves? . . . But it is from us and our labor that everything comes with which they maintain their pomp.[3]

Eventually the country priest inspired the peasants to a revolution against his oppressive government. The peasants followed political leaders like Jack Straw and Wat Tyler, who forced King Richard II to negotiate with them. The king promised to end serfdom and the oppressive taxes that inspired many to revolt. But when the peasants, satisfied that their demands were met, dispersed to their homes, the king reneged on his promises and declared, "serfs you were, and serfs you will remain." The leaders of the uprising, including the young priest, were executed, and the revolution failed.[4] Had Ball lived four hundred years later and a continent away, he would have been remembered as one of our great founding fathers, for his message was no different from that of the spokespersons for the American Revolution.

John Ball in 1381 read and perceived the implications of Genesis 1 concerning the man and the woman made in the image of God. Why did not more clergy discover this message in the Bible, and why did it take almost two thousand years for democracy to emerge in a Christian culture that supposedly used the Bible as its primary source for theology, ethics, worship, and Christian faith? Why do not all Christians today see this message of universal human equality and the concomitant concept of the equality of men and women? Is it because we quote the Bible but do not really read it? Though scholars comment on it in learned commentaries and scholarly articles, the egalitarian message has not yet infiltrated half of the churches in Christendom.

III

Gen 1:26-28 speaks to us of human equality, and it stands in reaction to the so-called superior status of kings that was lauded by so many ancient texts. This text is attributed to the Priestly editors who are dated to the sixth century B.C.E. or later. This text affirms human equality more dramatically than any text heretofore considered. It arose at a time when the Jews were a defeated nation and virtual prisoners of war as a people in the midst of Babylon, or under later Persian rule. To assault the institution of kingship and perhaps the ancient ideology of kingship while living under foreign rule was an act of intellectual courage and defiance. Herein we see the centuries-long criticism of kings among Israelite and later Jewish intelligentsia coming to fruition in a dramatic narrative.

Gen 1:26-28 inspired John Ball to lead the English Peasants' Revolt in 1381, and his observations of the equality of the man and the general equality of all people strike us as a very modern interpretation. But if he saw it in the text in the fourteenth century, then it is not our imagination that leads us to see it today.

According to Gen 1:26-28 God made both the man and the woman (not just the man, as some people seem to think) in the divine "image" and "likeness" and gave them the power to "rule" and have "dominion" over the world:

> [26]Then God said, "Let us make humankind in our image, according to our likeness; and let them have dominion over the fish of the sea, and over the birds of the air, and over the cattle, and over all the wild animals of the earth, and over every creeping thing that creeps

upon the earth." [27]So God created humankind in his image, in the image of God he created them; male and female he created them. [28]God blessed them, and God said to them, "Be fruitful and multiply, and fill the earth and subdue it; and have dominion over the fish of the sea and over the birds of the air and over every living thing that moves upon the earth."

In the ancient Near East terminology such as the "image" of the god or the "likeness" of the god were metaphors used to characterize the king, especially in Mesopotamia, where the king was the representative of the gods upon the earth. This language was used in order to legitimate the power of the kings.[5] Literally, in Mesopotamia, the terms "image" and "likeness" meant statues, and the implication was that the king was the visible "likeness" of the deity upon the earth. Likewise, the king was said to "rule" or have "dominion" over both the world and his people, as it was given to him by the gods. In Egypt the pharaoh was said to be in the "likeness" of a specific deity according to various texts.[6] The powerful implication of this biblical language was that the man and the woman, who symbolized all of humanity, were said to be kings and queens.

If God was the divine sovereign of all of creation, then people, who were made in the "image of God," must be the viceroys of the divine sovereign. This image of being the viceroy or agent of the supreme god by virtue of being in the image of that god was a distinction claimed especially by the kings of Assyria in the eighth and seventh centuries B.C.E.[7] Biblical authors were familiar with this Assyrian usage, so the same point was made in Genesis 1 about all men and women.

In the artistic conventions of the Assyrians it was common to show the king hunting wild animals, especially lions. This symbolically portrayed the king as protector of the civilized world against the wild forces of nature, most dramatically imagined as wild lions. Assyrian wall carvings often pictured Assyrian kings hunting lions. When God commissioned people to "rule" over animals and the whole creation, this was the same imagery as was attributed to the Assyrian king when he ruled wild animals to protect people.[8]

Hence, old concepts were democratized by the biblical text, for all humans were in the image of God, as kings once had been extolled. This major shift in ideology moved from old traditional royal ideologies to a new egalitarian one in which common people were elevated to the status of kings and perhaps even to the old mythic semidivine status once accorded to kings. Perhaps, the author of Genesis 1 may have become disillusioned with kings and wished to view God's direct activity in the world as manifest through all people, not just the select, chosen rulers.[9]

People, not kings, rule the entire earth on behalf of God.[10] Such appears to be the implication of Psalm 8, a text related to Genesis 1, which spoke of people being only a little less than God or the gods. In this particular Psalm we again observe that dominion was given to people, for in vv. 6-8 we read:

> [6]You [God] have given them dominion over the works of your hands; you have put all things under their feet, [7]all sheep and oxen, and also the beasts of the field, [8]the birds of the air, and the fish of the sea, whatever passes along the paths of the seas.

The words of this text evoked the memory of the language in Gen 1:26. Psalm 8 departed radically from the other royal psalms in the Psalter, for the authority of kings was attributed to people, who were the viceroys of God—kingship was democratized in this text as in Genesis 1.[11]

Perhaps such a new reconfiguration became possible in the exilic and postexilic era for Jewish intellectuals, once their own institution of kingship had disappeared.[12] This gave tremendous dignity and responsibility to all human beings. Their responsibilities entailed protection of the land; they were not to struggle with the created order, but they were to struggle to protect the created order. Previously, such was seen to be the task of kings. In Egypt, particularly, the pharaoh was responsible for defending the fertile agricultural land against the chaos of the creeping desert. In Genesis 1 such responsibility was entrusted to all human beings.[13]

IV

This theme was furthered in Genesis 2 where the man and the woman were placed into the garden. The ancient Near East knew of the imagery of a king in the sacred garden. At Mari, a city in Mesopotamia, we discovered a wall fresco from the early second millennium B.C.E. wherein the king was pictured in a garden, where he was invested as the king. The garden was watered by four streams and guarded by cherubim. The parallel with Genesis 2 is obvious.[14]

The creation of gardens was another prerogative of Mesopotamian kings who brought plants and animals from all over their empire and placed them into special royal gardens. In addition, the metaphor of the king's garden was applied to the king's rule over his empire. The king turned the entire land into his garden by wise rule. In Genesis 2 Yahweh was clearly the king who created such a garden for divine pleasure. But then Genesis 2 also attributed some ruling function to the man and the woman as representatives of all humanity.[15] The man named the animals and thus engaged in an important creative function, even though scholars debate the degree to which this made the man a cocreator with God.[16] His naming of the animals, however, signified his importance in ordering the garden, which made him appear to perform a function similar to the role of kings as gardeners for the gods. If we take the image from Mesopotamian political mythology, we may metaphor Yahweh as the king, or we may view Yahweh as the high god and the man (and woman) then represent the king on earth who does the bidding of the gods.

Critical scholarship assumes that the account in Genesis 2 is older than that of Genesis 1. It may come from the preexilic period or perhaps from the early exile. In its original form Genesis 2 may not have had the idea of portraying the man as a king, but rather as a being who lived in harmonious relationship to Yahweh and worked with Yahweh. When the later text in Genesis 1 was added by Priestly authors, however, the democratizing of royal epitaphs in Genesis 1 made the reader more prone to see the image of the garden in Genesis 2 as a royal park, Yahweh as the king who created the garden, and the man (and woman) as sharing in those royal attributes of creation and rule. If the suggestion in the previous paragraph is correct, then Genesis 1 may lead the reader to view the scene in Genesis 2 as follows: Eden is the royal garden of the world, Yahweh represents the pantheon of Mesopotamian gods, and the man and the woman rule the garden as king and queen.

These were all powerful statements to make in the ancient world where the assumption of the great cultures was that the king (or pharaoh) was either divine, as in Egypt where pharaoh was Horus and the son of Osiris, or a representative of the gods who could be adopted as divine, as in Mesopotamia. The biblical text declared that every man and every woman were equal to the king and obviously equal to each other. If the text in Genesis 1 came from priests in the exile or later, their revolutionary egalitarian statements were uttered under foreign rule. To me this reflects not only deep religious faith in Yahweh but also significant intellectual courage.

Genesis 1–3 contained the core creation accounts of the Bible. When this narrative concluded, the man and the woman had names, Adam and Eve, lived outside the garden, and began the world's first family by giving birth to Cain and Abel. While biblical creation accounts culminated with the origin of the first family, comparable Mesopotamian stories concluded with the creation of the state, and of course, the institution of kingship. This is yet another example of the subtle parody on kingship.[17]

V

In Genesis 4 Cain went to the land of Nod, in the east, after killing his brother and receiving the mark of protection from God. Often commentators assume that Cain went to the land of the Transjordan, which is east of Israel. But the biblical author may have pointed even further east, to the land of Mesopotamia, where the ancients lived (including those who built the tower of Babel). Mesopotamia would be a good candidate, because great cities were in that river valley, and the text spoke of how Cain founded a city. Our biblical author elsewhere hinted that the earliest cities were in Mesopotamia or Shinar. If the reference to the east hinted at Mesopotamia as the land of cities, we may observe the sarcasm of the biblical author. The first murderer went to Mesopotamia, the land that sent murderous armies from Assyria and Chaldean Babylon to destroy the people of Israel. Cain "invented" cities, cities that were the source of human pride, greed, and oppression. Perhaps we also sense the biblical author's antipathy toward cities, with their kings and their priests, who ruled in tyrannical fashion. The tyranny of the cities in Mesopotamia was a theme throughout the Primeval History.

VI

In the ancient *Sumerian King List* there were a number of heroes who lived before the flood for thousands of years, and who functioned as kings over the antediluvian peoples.[18] The biblical text responded with its own list and antediluvian figures, the two lists of the descendents of Cain (Gen 4:17-25) and Seth (Gen 5:1-32). (Interestingly enough both biblical lists contain the same names, perhaps implying that we are the descendents of both the bad Cainites and the good Sethites, which means we are a combination of good and evil.) But for our purposes it should be noted that none of the biblical personages lived more than a thousand years;

only Methuselah came close with 969 years. The point of the biblical author was that these personages died "young" because they were not divine or semidivine kings, as the Mesopotamians claimed. If you live for more than one thousand years you must be divine or semidivine. The youngest of the Mesopotamian heroes died at thirty-six thousand years. The subtle undercurrent in the text was that later Mesopotamian kings, who ruled when the literary texts were used as propaganda, shared at least in the semidivine status, even if the longevity were lost. The ancients often claimed divine status for their kings. This, of course, undergirded their political authority. In response, the biblical text declared that the antediluvian personages were mortal and died "young," and thus none of them were gods or semidivine. Furthermore, the biblical personages were not even kings but apparently simple pastoralists. From this perspective the biblical text undermined the ideology of kingship by denying the royal and semidivine status of the so-called earliest kings.[19] When modern readers of the Bible ask why did these biblical figures live so long, the answer is that they really lived "short" lives because they were simply mortal, not divine or semidivine tyrannical kings.

VII

A person of interest in the list is Enoch, the seventh patriarchal figure, who walked with God and was taken by God, or translated to heaven. This reminds us of Elijah, who also was taken to heaven alive in a whirlwind accompanied by a fiery chariot. The usual interpretation is that Enoch was taken alive into the heavenly realm without dying, though there are some references to his death. This assumption into heaven, of course, gave rise to great speculation in the Jewish tradition, so that by the second century B.C.E. Enoch was envisioned as a great seer and wise sage who was drawn up into the heavenly realm and permitted to see the future. His visions of the future emerged in several writings, most of which were drawn together in the book of Enoch (we call it 1 Enoch). Other literature that bore his name also developed out of a complex set of traditions about this heavenly seer. Enoch was mentioned in documents from Qumran from the second century B.C.E., including some fragments of 1 Enoch. In the Apocryphal or Deuterocanonical book of Sirach, Enoch's perfection was mentioned (Sir 44:16), and in the Apocryphal or Deuterocanonical Wisdom of Solomon, Enoch was the example of a righteous man in whom the wisdom of the age came to fruition during his youth (even though he died). In the New Testament, Enoch was seen as a man of faith who did not die (Heb 11:5-6).

Enoch lived for 365 years before God took him according to Gen 5:22-24, and that is the number of days in a year. This prompts scholars to compare him to Enmeduranna or Enmeduranki who was listed in the *Sumerian King List*. Both personages were seventh in their succession of antediluvian heroes. Enmeduranna, the Sumerian, taught divinatory rites by the sun god, and his adviser, Utuabzu (who was seventh on a list of antediluvian sages) was said to have ascended to heaven.[20] This is too much similarity to be a coincidence. Enoch seems to have combined characteristics of both Mesopotamian figures.

The figure of Enoch spoofed the Mesopotamian king Enmeduranna who was a king with great wisdom obtained from the sun God; Enoch was a wise sage (at least according to later Jewish literature), who had a prominent place in heaven (also according to later Jewish tradition), but he was not a king. Perhaps this is another critique of kingship. It is likely that there is more biblical critique of Mesopotamian belief involved here, but we have to guess at what it was. (Perhaps, because Israelites had been prone to worship the sun as a deity, and both Israelites and even later Jews were tempted to equate Yahweh with the sun,[21] this story was meant to critique sun veneration in some way.)

VIII

The beginning of the flood account has a strange narrative about how the "sons of God" or "sons of the gods" came down and had sex with the "daughters of men" (Gen 6:2). The text said that "nephilim" were on the earth when the "sons of God" had children by the "daughters of men" and these were the heroes of renown (Gen 6:4). These "heroes of renown" may have referred to the nephilim or to the children birthed by the "daughters of men," or the text most likely may have meant that the nephilim were children born to the "daughters of men" and they were also the "heroes of renown." The implication of the ensuing narrative about the flood was that the birth of these individuals was one of the reasons for the flood.

Who were these "sons of God" or "sons of the gods"? Biblical interpreters suggest three opinions on this matter. Some believe the "sons of God" were the descendants of Seth, while the "daughters of men" were the descendants of Cain. Some believe that they were heavenly beings who

mated with human beings to produce children of mixed divine and
human heritage, like the Babylonian epic hero Gilgamesh, who was two-
thirds divine and one-third human. Such heroes were praised in the myths
of ancient Near Easterners. In this case, our biblical author may not have
believed that such activities occurred, but rather our author sought to
ridicule the stories of contemporaries in the ancient world who praised
such individuals as heroes and the ancestors of their nations. The critique
came with the biblical author's implication that the birth of such heroes
was evil and caused the flood. "So much for your ancestors, they caused
only destruction!" said the biblical author. There is a third interpretative
possibility, which I like. Some believe that the "sons of God" or the "sons
of the gods" were kings in the ancient Near East who claimed to be divine—great Mesopotamian rulers, like the epic figure Gilgamesh, who
claimed the right to have initial sex with any women recently married.
Since Gilgamesh was said to be two-thirds divine, an ancient wonder of
genetic engineering, he would be a "son of the gods." Kings in Mesopotamia often claimed divine status, using the expression "dinger" in their
titles, which implied divinity. Such kings brought the destruction of the
flood upon us. Furthermore, Gen 6:4 referred to the heroes of "renown,"
or men of great name. This reminds us of Genesis 11 wherein the builders
of the tower sought to make a name for themselves (Gen 11:4). Even
though kings were not mentioned in Genesis 11, the hint of royal authority was there. "Making a name for oneself" was what Mesopotamian
kings did by their wars and building projects. The allusion to "renown"
and "making a name" in these two stories seems to hint strongly at the
activities of kings, especially when combined with the themes of the royal
right of sex with any women in Genesis 6 and the building project in
Genesis 11.[22] If this is a correct interpretation, then Gen 6:1-4 and Gen
11:1-9 are both about the arrogant pride of kings, who claimed to be divine
and with their overweening royal pride usurped the prerogatives of God.
In both stories God struck them down for their pride.

IX

The ending to the biblical account of the flood contained critiques of
Mesopotamian kingship. This was true of the Yahwist ending in Gen
8:21-22 and the Priestly conclusion to the expanded flood narrative in
Gen 9:1-17 both of which recalled God's promise not to flood the world.
The entire biblical account of the flood was a parody on Mesopotamian

beliefs in many ways, especially the narratives about Ziusudra, Atrahasis, and Utnapishtim—the various Babylonian Noahs. But the flood conclusion attacked Mesopotamian kingship in particular ways.

(1) The Mesopotamians engaged in complex religious rites at the New Year *Akiti* or *Akitu* festival, led by their priests and the king, to avoid another flood. By these rituals they gave strength to Marduk, the god of Babylon, to defeat the power of chaos, the evil goddess of water, Tiamat, every year and thus to avert the destruction of Babylon by floods. The possible reenactment of this drama, which may have featured the king annually in the role of Marduk, gave tremendous psychological legitimation to the king as the representative of the divine realm. When the biblical narrative declared that a flood would never happen again, it made the Babylonians and their king look foolish with this superfluous ritual. (2) The hero of the flood in one account, Ziusudra, was a king. His reception of the gift of immortality for surviving the flood added credibility to the divine status of the king. (Atrahasis and Utnapishtim also received immortality in their versions of the account.) In the biblical account, however, Noah was not a king and he received no immortality after the flood; rather, the blessing of God was for all people—the curse on the ground was removed (Gen 8:21) and people were enabled to eat meat (Gen 9:2-4), as well as the promise of no more flood. This further debunked the status of primordial heroes who could be seen as ancient kings.

X

The symbolic story of the building of the tower of Babel in Genesis 11 was another antiroyal account. The sin of the tower builders was their desire to storm the heavens to make a name for themselves, which symbolically meant that they sought to invade the divine realm and become immortal like the gods. Thus, they averted the destruction of another flood sent by the gods, or they avoided being scattered by Yahweh (v. 4). Put in other terms, the sin of the builders was tremendous pride, the desire to be like the gods, which in the opinion of biblical authors was the sin of the Mesopotamian kings.

Mesopotamian kings considered it one of their chief duties to build temple ziggurats in their cities. Mesopotamian ziggurats were cosmic mountains that reached to the heavens, and the worshiping individuals—the king and priests who could build and ascend such mountains—had their authority on this world legitimated by such activity.

Great ziggurats were built by Ur-Nammu in Ur (2000 B.C.E.), Hammurabi in Babylon (1750 B.C.E.), and Nebuchadnezzar I in Babylon (1100
B.C.E.). Of special interest is the temple ziggurat, the Entemenanki, in
Babylon, which was built by the Assyrian king Esarhaddon in the mid-
seventh century B.C.E., rebuilt by the Chaldean Babylonian king Nabo-
pollasar in the late seventh century B.C.E., and refurbished by two
Chaldean Babylonian kings, Nebuchadnezzar II and Nabonidus, in the
early and mid-sixth century B.C.E. In his royal inscriptions Nebuchadnezzar bragged about building the Entemenanki, the cosmic mountain
where the gods dwelt, and using laborers drawn from all parts of the
empire.[23] Those peoples obviously included Jews exiled after the destruction of Jerusalem in 586 B.C.E. Genesis 11 may be a parody on the building efforts of Nebuchadnezzar. In his inscription he declared:

> I called into me the far dwelling peoples over whom Marduk my
> lord had appointed me and whose care was given unto me by
> Shamash the hero, from all lands and of every inhabited place from
> the upper sea to the lower sea from distant lands the people of far
> away habitations kings of distant mountains and remote regions
> who dwell at the upper and the nether seas with whose strength
> Marduk the lord has filled my hands that they should bear his yoke
> and also the subjects of Shamash and Marduk I summoned to build
> Entemenanki.[24]

Nebuchadnezzar and his temple in Babylon would be a great candidate
for the parody in Genesis because he was the ruler who destroyed Jerusalem in 586 B.C.E. and dragged the Jews into exile. Another possibility,
however, is the last Chaldean ruler of Babylon, Nabonidus. Nabonidus
built shrines in Ur, Babylon, and Haran (550 B.C.E.). Notice how Abraham moved through the three cities in which Nabonidus built his shrines
and temples. Also, Nabonidus built to the honor of Sin, the moon god,
and Abraham's family was portrayed as worshipers of the moon. Nabonidus was a Chaldean, and Abraham came from Ur of the Chaldees.
It appears that the Abraham accounts may parody the times of Nabonidus, ruler during the Babylonian Exile, so that Abraham became a symbol
of returning exiles after 539 B.C.E. For after the Babel story Abram was
called forth from Ur of the "Chaldees" to go to Palestine (Gen 11:27-31;
12:1-9), just as the Jews did in the years after 539 B.C.E.

In response to such Mesopotamian imagery and obvious architectural
propaganda, the biblical author painted a story of human pride and
divine punishment to ridicule such Babylonian pretensions to power

and self-proclaimed divinity. Yahweh came down to the tower, the zig-gurat, the cosmic mountain, and scattered the builders by confusing their language. Yahweh came down to view the tower not because he lost his bifocals, but because the tower was too small to be seen from the heavens. This was humorous satire by the biblical author on how truly insignifi-cant the so-called great works of the Babylonian kings really were. Actu-ally, this story may be veiled commentary on the fact that slave labor from many different parts of the empire would have been used to con-struct such a temple ziggurat. Subsequently, with the fall of Chaldean Babylon to Cyrus of Persia in 540 B.C.E., work on various shrines and temples under the direction of Nabonidus ceased, and the slave peoples, including the Jews, were permitted to return to their homes, or they were allowed to "scatter," as was the will of Yahweh in the first place. Not only was the account a commentary on Nabonidus and the return of the Jews in the sixth century B.C.E., but it was critical satire on the policies of Mesopotamian kings in general. (Nabonidus may also be spoofed as the insane king Nebuchadnezzar in Daniel 4, so that the later biblical tradition recalled the specific critique against him, but transferred them to the more well-known Nebuchadnezzar. Both Babylonian and Persian texts recalled Nabonidus' insanity to explain why Babylon fell.)

XI

The Primeval History contained powerful symbolic narratives func-tioning with many levels of meaning. The most important was the con-trast of human finitude or sinfulness with divine grace. Equally important was Yahweh's progressive work with people in an attempt to find a harmonious relationship with the creatures, which finally led to the election of a particular people in Abraham. But one of the important motifs that ran through the narratives was the critique of kings, and especially the arrogant claims of kings in Mesopotamia.

I do not seek to reject other interpretations and approaches to Genesis 1–11, but I do believe these texts are polyvalent, that is, they carry many levels of meaning and religious truth. I believe we have not focused sufficiently on the egalitarian themes: the proclamation of human equal-ity and the repudiation of kingship with all the ideational and social values connected to that institution in the ancient world.

10. Novellas

Within the Bible there are a number of literary works that scholars call "novellas," short stories that have a well-defined plot and vivid characterization of the main figures involved in the story. Often the plotline develops because of the decisions and actions of the characters, and God is somewhat distant. Hence, these stories contrast with the more dramatic epic materials found in Genesis and Exodus, as well as much of the material in the Deuteronomistic History. Often these short stories are found as one complete biblical book, but they can be part of a larger biblical book, as is the case with the Joseph Novella in Genesis 37, 39–50 and the Succession Narrative in 2 Samuel 9–20; 1 Kings 1–2. Classic short stories or novellas include Ruth, Esther, Jonah, Daniel 1–6, Additions to Daniel, Tobit, and Judith. One can discern the ridicule or condemnation of kings in the Joseph Novella, Daniel, Esther, and Judith, and these deserve our consideration.

I

Joseph faithfully served Pharaoh in the narrative found in those later chapters of Genesis. But when we look closely at Joseph's interpretation of Pharaoh's dreams, we find some definite indications that Pharaoh was not the divine incarnation of the god Horus, as Egyptians claimed he was. In fact, he did not seem wise in any way. As we read in Gen 41:1-8 Pharaoh had two dreams, one about cows and the other about corn. He could not interpret them, nor could the wise men of his court, and thus it remained for the Hebrew boy, Joseph, to interpret them (Gen 41:9-36). Significantly, Joseph declared that God will interpret the dream,

not himself (v. 16), thus implying that he was a prophet, not a professional oneirocritic, or dream interpreter, as Pharaoh's servants were. This
sounds like an insult to the professionals who served Pharaoh and,
maybe by inference, an insult to kings in general.

II

This essential plotline is repeated in the book of Daniel both in chapters
2 and 4. In Dan 2:1-16 King Nebuchadnezzar had a dream, called his wise
men to interpret it, but then demanded that they tell him what he dreamed
in addition to interpreting. His demand was comical but also illustrated
the tyrannical nature of royalty, for he decreed that he would have them
torn limb from limb and their families killed unless they did this (v. 6).
Daniel, like Joseph before him, came to the rescue and interpreted the
dream as well as recounting it for the king (Dan 2:17-45). The violence
intended by the irrational monarch did not occur—a happy ending for
all concerned. Again, in Dan 4:1-37 the king had a dream, the wise men
failed once more (they should have sought other employment), but Daniel
came forth to properly interpret the dream. One gets the impression that
the king and his professional interpreters were rather inept. Ultimately
Daniel 4 described how King Nebuchadnezzar was punished for his arrogance, for the dream predicted that he would go insane for a period of
time, and he did. The king dreamed that he was a great tree, a frequent
metaphor used in ancient texts to describe how rulers protected and gave
fertility to the world.[1] But the tree in this dream was cut down, and that
was interpreted by Daniel to mean that Nebuchadnezzar would go insane,
a fitting punishment for a king who envisioned himself as a cosmic tree
with something akin to cosmic vanity. He would roam in the wilderness
as a wild animal, eating grass, with long hair and uncut fingernails. We
are reminded of one of our own modern-day Nebuchadnezzars, a rich
and powerful man, Howard Hughes, who late in his life became an insane
recluse with long hair and fingernails also. Our modern kings are the
powerful investors and financiers, the stockbrokers, moneylenders, and
mortgage brokers, and these Nebuchadnezzars likewise go insane, especially when their paper empire of Wall Street collapses, so that they re-
spond by leaping out of their tall office buildings. Upon regaining his
sanity, Nebuchadnezzar praised the God of the Jews. He did not jump
out of a building, nor did he appear before congress and deny any ac-
countability for his bogus manipulation of wealth and peoples' lives.

Nebuchadnezzar comes off looking better than a number of folk who appear before congressional hearings.

In sum, the story was one about royal arrogance and its corresponding punishment, yet again another critique of kings who were drunk with their power.[2] By appealing to this story Andrew Melville reminded James VI, king of Scotland, that Scotland had another king, God, and in God's kingdom even James VI was a subject, and James VI must acknowledge that.[3] This is truly the message of Daniel 4.

How significant is it that we have in the Bible a powerful statement of praise uttered to God by the evil King Nebuchadnezzar, who conquered Jerusalem in historical time (586 B.C.E.)? Does it not plant the idea in the minds of readers that even kings pale before the power of God if they do evil? Does it not say that evil kings ultimately must be punished or brought down from their thrones, as Nebuchadnezzar was turned into a wild beast for a time? Listen to the words of Nebuchadnezzar in Dan 4:34-35:

> [34]When that period was over, I, Nebuchadnezzar, lifted my eyes to heaven, and my reason returned to me. I blessed the Most High, and praised and honored the one who lives forever. For his sovereignty is an everlasting sovereignty, and his kingdom endures from generation to generation. [35]All the inhabitants of the earth are accounted as nothing, and he does what he wills with the host of heaven and the inhabitants of the earth. There is no one who can stay his hand or say to him, "What are you doing?"

The author of the book of Daniel knew that kings too often forgot that they were creatures and not semidivine beings, as royal propaganda would have it. They must be reminded of their creaturely status. Nebuchadnezzar had to be given a good lesson concerning the contingent nature of human kingship; he had to learn that kings have their power derived from the will of God. The humiliation and repentant response of Nebuchadnezzar was a powerful image by our biblical author of how kings need to be brought to an awareness of their real place in this world.[4]

The book of Daniel has other stories that portray the king in more sinister fashion. King Nebuchadnezzar set up a golden statue and demanded that people worship it or be thrown into a fiery furnace (Dan 3:1-7). This, of course, was a symbolic commentary on how Antiochus IV Epiphanes, a Seleucid (Greek Syrian) ruler, set up a statue in the temple precincts of Jerusalem in 167 B.C.E. and demanded that Jews worship it under pain of death. In the Daniel account, Shadrach,

Meshach, and Abednego were found guilty of failing to worship the statue and were thrown into the fiery furnace, but they survived in wondrous fashion and the king took them out of the furnace and elevated their status in his kingdom (Dan 3:8-30). When the king first heard that the Jewish boys refused to revere his statue, "the king falls into the typical rage of the Oriental tyrant whose will is thwarted."[5] But their dramatic survival in the furnace bent his iron will to acknowledge their God (v. 28) and set them free. Such a turn of events was the hoped-for goal in the minds of many biblical authors, not only for foreign kings, but also for their own rulers who were puppets of those foreign kings. This is a story about the arrogance and folly of a king in promoting idolatry. How tragic it is that the fiery furnace foreshadows the ovens of the Holocaust in World War II, where once more Jews were thrown in and burned.[6] At that time, also, it was the will of a tyrant, Adolph Hitler, to destroy a helpless people. The story of the three men in the fiery furnace is not a children's tale or cute Sunday school story; it is a parable of human intolerance and brutality led by tyrants who continue to cross the stage of history.

Belshazzar had a feast in which he abused the sacred vessels of the Jewish temple by using them to party. In so doing, he truly behaved as a "frivolous character" and not in the manner that kings ought to act.[7] A hand appeared and wrote a strange message on the wall that only Daniel could interpret. Yet again the court magicians and wise men failed to interpret the message. One wonders why the royal family did not fire this rather incompetent lot. (They must have had tenure.) Daniel interpreted this word of judgment to indicate that the Babylonian Empire would fall to the Medes and the Persians, which happened very quickly (Dan 5:1-30). Again, folly and arrogance of a king brought about his demise, for the text declared that he died the very night Daniel interpreted the message (v. 30). The entire narrative spoke of inadequate royal leadership and the need for change. Sibley Tower suggests that the story may be, in part, a commentary on the behavior of Antiochus IV Epiphanes, who persecuted the Jews so badly in the years 167–164 B.C.E., for he engaged in raucous behavior at royal feasts and on public occasions.[8] Such is the behavior of those in power; they believe that they stand above the everyday moral norms that other people abide by. A local politician in my neighborhood was arrested by police in his home late one night. The charges were fraud and misuse of public funds. When they arrived they found him entertained by a nightclub lap dancer performing for him in his living room—obviously paid for with public funds! Such is the way of behaving when leaders believe themselves to be above the law.

Commentators also have pointed out the similarity of Belshazzar's folly and abuse of power with the actions of David in seducing Bathsheba and killing Uriah (1 Sam 11:1-27), and also the arrogant actions of Rehoboam in alienating the northern tribes of Israel (1 Kgs 12:1-20). In all these instances the king acted so as to demonstrate his deep down belief that he could do as he pleased because he was the king. In all three stories the king was justly brought down. It is also likely that the story of Belshazzar was actually a veiled narrative on the historical actions of a Seleucid king, Antiochus IV Epiphanes, who looted the Jerusalem temple in 169 B.C.E. to defray the expenses of his wars.[9] (That was two years before he set up the idol in the temple and demanded that Jews worship it.)

A modern story of Belshazzar's feast comes to us from Iran in the early 1970s. In October 1971 the shah of Iran invited six hundred internationally rich and powerful guests to a banquet to celebrate the 2,500th anniversary of the founding of the Persian Empire. Under a ceiling of expensive silk the guests experienced a five-hour meal with quail eggs stuffed with caviar, roast peacock served in its own plumage, and the most expensive wine. The larger celebration lasted for four days. Guests included one emperor, eight kings, a cardinal, grand dukes, crown prices, sheiks, presidents, premiers, and vice presidents (the United States sent Spiro Agnew). Less than ten years later the shah was deposed by popular riots, exiled, and dead—how strikingly similar to the fate of Belshazzar. How ephemeral is worldly glory![10]

In Dan 6:1-5 we discover that Daniel was one of the favorite counselors of the Persian king, Darius. Darius was advised by other counselors, who were intensely jealous of Daniel, that all the subjects in his kingdom should pray only to the king for thirty days, or else be thrown into a den of lions, and so Darius signed the document to make it so (Dan 6:6-9). That any king would do this is comic arrogance. The royal advisors convinced the king that it was for the good of the nation that he be worshiped. He was really a "puppet" in the hands of his advisors, who had their own agenda.[11]

A tyrant in his pride and arrogance can so easily become the tool of those around him. He is so easily manipulated by his vanity, his overweening ego, and his desire for raw power. The king is trapped by his own vices. For such is the folly of kings, and sometimes even democratically elected presidents. How many leaders in our world would fall prey to this kind of advice in our own age? I am reminded of all the statues and pictures of Chairman Mao of China erected and posted in a past generation and how the students so reverently quoted the "Blue Book" of Mao as though it were a sacred text. How many dictators of small countries develop a god complex? Sometimes the smaller the country is, the greater the god complex of the leader becomes. These leaders, of course, think that they do this for the "good" of the nation.

Our biblical author was playing this story in extreme fashion, for no historical Persian king would have done this. Our author again parodied the arrogance of Antiochus IV Epiphanes because of his brutal persecution of Jews from 167 to 164 B.C.E. Daniel, of course, disobeyed the decree (stubborn little Jewish believer), and he was thrown into the lion's den. God prevented the lions from eating Daniel. So upon discovering that Daniel was still alive the next day, Darius ordered the counselors and their entire families to be thrown into the lion's den to be consumed by lions who were even more hungry now and presumably quite cranky from having their mouths shut by God all night long. The king appeared incredibly vain to have desired such worship, and how stupid was he not to find out ahead of time that his favorite counselor would break the decree. Always check out all the ramifications of the decisions that you make or some unforeseen result will burn you! Good advice for everyone, but especially for those in charge of other people.

A final story about Daniel comes from a chapter that was added to the book very late, and thus is found only in the Greek translation of Daniel, called the Septuagint, but not in the Hebrew Old Testament. Some modern English translations that end with Daniel 12 may include several Daniel stories as separate accounts in the Apocrypha. (Daniel 1–12 may have arisen in Palestine as a written document, and when it went to Egypt, perhaps then Daniel 13–14 was added.) In Dan 14:1-27 we are told that Cyrus the Persian asked Daniel to worship Bel, the statue of a Babylonian god. (This is another name for the Babylonian god Marduk, the deity who created the world.) This little tale was an "idol parody" or a "confrontation tale" in which the hero, Daniel, opposed a deity or an idol and won because he represented the one true God.[12] In this tale the king was convinced that Bel was a real god because the food placed before him was consumed overnight. But Daniel unveiled for the king the secret—the Babylonian priests came up through a trapdoor in the floor and took the food. Daniel dropped ashes on the floor so that the priests left footprints overnight. The king had been played for a fool, but Daniel, with his wisdom, saved the day. Daniel appears to be an ancient

Sherlock Holmes, and he should have been as abrasive with the king as Holmes was with Watson.

Throughout the book of Daniel, both in the short and longer form, we have stories that portray kings as foolish and tyrannical. Accounts in Daniel 1–2, 4, 14 reflected a general attitude toward kings; accounts in Daniel 3, 5–6 reflected the attitude of Jews after their experience of the Maccabean persecution in 167–164 B.C.E. But in all the stories the kings were portrayed as fools.

III

The book of Esther tells us about another Jew in the court of a foreign king, a pattern that we can observe with stories about Joseph, Daniel, and Esther, as well as other popular Jewish romances from the era of 500 B.C.E. to 100 C.E. In the book of Esther the king was Ahasuerus, a fictional name for any theoretic Persian king in the era of 550 to 330 B.C.E. He was fop and a fool. He gave a huge party with extensive drinking that lasted for days (Esth 1:1-9). On the seventh day, after innumerable bottles of wine, he decided to show off the beauty of his wife Vashti, but she refused (Esth 1:10-12). (Seven days of drinking! That was no time to be making executive decisions!) This refusal to appear was an impressive display of courage on her part, especially in response to the great Persian king, who was called the "king of kings, and Lord of Lords" in royal inscriptions. Her refusal caused a panic, because it might inspire other women to stand up to their husbands and thus bring chaos to the empire. (Oh my, a feminist movement in the Persian Empire!) So the king deposed Vashti and sent out a decree to his entire empire declaring that every man must remain the master in his own home (Esth 1:13-22). (I'm sure that all the men folk were very relieved to hear this. The empire put the brakes on all the uppity women.) Thus, the crisis was averted. Yes, this story was meant to be comical! But also notice how the king and his counselors were thrown into a panic because of the bold refusal of one woman. It does seem as though the king was being ridiculed, along with all of his august advisors!

Commentators frequently have pointed out that the king and his court structures were ridiculed as ineffective by the resistance of one woman, Vashti.[13] The king has "inordinate official power but no moral strength" and his entire imperial administration appears "overblown, pompous, over-bureaucratized." The narrative was a farce on royal power.[14] This narrative placed the rest of the book into a grand comic relief. Ahasuerus rejected Vashti's insubordination and squashed it, yet he later deferred to his new wife, Esther (Esth 5:6; 7:2; 9:12), until finally he followed her advice to execute Haman and allowed Jews to defend themselves against a brutal pogrom. It appears that the king could control his wealth and display it to his friends (Esth 1:1-9), but he could not control a human being, especially a wife.[15] Ultimately, the king was manipulated by other people who appealed to his self-love, his honor, and his anxiety over his own authority.[16] How many executive decisions have been made by leaders over the years for precisely those very same reasons? A classic example of this occurred when Haman came to Ahasuerus and declared (Esth 3:8-9):

> [8]There is a certain people scattered and separated among the peoples in all the provinces of your kingdom; their laws are different from those of every other people, and they do not keep the king's laws, so that it is not appropriate for the king to tolerate them. [9]If it pleases the king, let a decree be issued for their destruction, and I will pay ten thousand talents of silver into the hands of those who have charge of the king's business, so that they may put it into the king's treasuries.

Did the king even bother to ask who these people were? Did he bother to ask whether it would affect anyone known to him? Did he bother to ask whether genocide would be bad for the political welfare of his kingdom? No! He signed the decree on the basis of his advisor's opinion and because the magic words were "they do not keep the king's law." They were said to challenge his authority and hence his vanity. So they must die. Is this not the way of kings and tyrants? How many times has something like this happened even in our modern era? How often do bad decisions get made high in the circles of political power because a handful of people advise a leader to undertake a course of action in an atmosphere of "groupthink" wherein no one challenges the opinion of the few key advisors, least of all the political leader? How often do such "groupthink" decisions lead to war or the destruction of people's lives because of the lack of restraint in those ruling circles and the loss of common sense?

Some commentators have noticed that there might be a comparison between king Ahasuerus and Mordecai, the good uncle of Esther, who helped her throughout the book. At one point, Mordecai was honored by the Persian king when he rode on the royal horse and wore royal regalia (Esth 6:8; 8:15). This was an unusual honor; Mordecai was portrayed as though he were king and not the real king. Perhaps, this was Jewish humor—the humble Jew, Mordecai, received the fanfare due to the great king, implying that the king was not really any more important than Mordecai. This would be ultimate comic reversal. Others see the entire book of Esther playing with the image that perhaps Mordecai was more truly a king than Ahasuerus, since the biblical text hinted that Mordecai was descended from royal blood in Israel, namely Saul. The deeper contrast was between the ruling power of Persia and the conquered Jews.[17] We sense that the Jews, crushed underneath the boots of the oppressors, were the truly royal and noble people, not the conquering Persians. So, for a brief moment in Esth 6:8, the true king, and not the fop and fool, Ahasuerus, rode on the royal horse.

The rest of the book of Esther described how Haman plotted to kill the Jews, but Esther came forth before the king to admit that she was a Jew and that her people should not be slaughtered. There is much humor in the rest of the book obviously. But for our concerns, we notice how the king really was deceived by Haman, enlightened by Esther, and was very much in the dark about most of what was happening. Jon Levenson aptly notes that this novel deeply resonates the historic Israelite disdain for kingship.[18]

As a side observation, it is interesting to note that American authors immediately prior to the Revolutionary War occasionally appealed to the imagery in the book of Esther. They equated Haman, the evil counselor of the king, with Lord North, advisor to George III. Of course, the foppish king in the book of Esther was George III himself.[19] So even the book of Esther provided some direct ammunition for the founding fathers of our country.

IV

The book of Judith, which is found in the Greek Septuagint, but not the Hebrew Bible, is therefore one of those books placed in the Apocrypha by Protestants. It recounted how Judith saved her little city of Bethulia (perhaps a comic symbol of Jerusalem) against evil general Holofernes of Assyria (probably a comic symbol of the Seleucid rulers and their empire in the second century B.C.E.).[20] She consulted with the elders of her city, who were pretty worthless, and then went out with a basket of food to wine, dine, and presumably seduce Holofernes in his tent (Judith 8–12). There was no seduction, but she did chop off his head after he was drunk (Judith 13). (Never go on a picnic with Judith!) Granted, Holofernes was a general in this entertaining little tale, but in reality he symbolized royal authority and can be seen as a king. Like so many kings in the Bible, he was portrayed as a fool, with a weakness for women and wine, with the result that he lost his head, literally. The courage of Judith contrasted vividly with the cowering and trembling elders and others among her people who were so willing to surrender and not stand up for their faith.[21]

V

The novels, in general, have a more comic approach in their satire. Their primary message was to encourage Jews to stay faithful to their religion wherever they might find themselves, especially if it was in the court of the king. Joseph, Daniel, and Esther were in royal courts, Judith in a general's tent (close enough to a court, I suppose); they stood by their convictions and beliefs, and God led them to success. But a side theme seems to be the folly and tyrannical behavior of kings, and how God will be with the common Jew over against the powerful royal personage.

Throughout the novels we find common themes in the portrayal of kings. They were fools, and they were easily deceived by common people who had God on their side. In some instances, as with Holofernes, the commoners prevailed in physical combat and the king died. This is so diametrically opposed to the usual laudatory praise heaped on kings as great warriors in battle, the repositories of the wisdom of the gods, and the very presence of the divine in this world. As I have said repeatedly, we have become so familiar with these stories in Sunday school and in popular lore, we fail to appreciate their political innuendo. We have been unconsciously taught by the Bible that kings were no more special than any commoner, and, in fact, when the kings sided against the prophet or the will of God, they were defeated by the average person. If these stories are read and taught to children on a regular basis, you will raise up a great number of egalitarian revolutionaries. But then, I guess that is what we did in the last few centuries.

11. New Testament

I

In the New Testament we find comparable concepts as we have observed in the Old Testament, albeit residing in texts in a more subtle fashion. Early Christians in the first century C.E. wisely spread their message among the masses without provoking political persecution. Being persecuted for confessing Jesus as savior and refusing to worship the Roman emperor was a sufficient reason to die in the arena; they did not wish to go forth and provoke the state for other reasons. Their willingness to oppose Roman law on certain issues is evident, such as Paul's advice to Philemon. By encouraging Philemon not to punish his escaped slave, Onesimus, Paul was telling Philemon to break Roman law. But in general Christians were not about to engage in wholesale critique of the government in the manner of the Hebrew prophets. First of all, they believed that Jesus would return shortly, and he would bring judgment down on the oppressive Roman Empire. Second, they had not the power to effectively change their society, least of all, to remove kings and create a democratic society. They were the powerless people of the empire, and the Christian message appealed to so many of those powerless folk, for it spoke of a God who acted dramatically on their behalf. Early Christianity provided a hope to powerless people on another level of reality. Nor did they have the conceptual apparatus to envision a democratic society. That would come in time. As in the evolutionary process—the implications of a mutation in a species take time to unfold in the natural process—so also in the social realm; a great intellectual and religious breakthrough will take time for all of its implications to unfold and transform the social arena.[1]

The vast majority of people in the first century C.E. lived in abject poverty and oppression. Though modern textbooks might laud the accomplishments of the great Roman Empire, the benefits of the empire were enjoyed by only a few in the Mediterranean world. For too many people, especially Jews and the early Christians, the Roman Empire was an oppressive and crushing reality.

> The early Roman Empire . . . was a society where gleaming cities were rising in some places and children went hungry in others. It was a world where no luxury was enough for some great aristocrats and public celebrities, and where even the basic necessities of life lay beyond the grasp of the urban and rural poor. It was a world where dreams of limitless material wealth and technological progress danced in the heads of the great entrepreneurs and in the rhetoric of ambitious politicians—and where the looming nightmares of family breakdown, crime, sudden loss of livelihood, and untreated and untreatable illnesses plagued the minds of the vast majority. It was, in short, a world that should seem ominously familiar.[2]

Texts in the New Testament reflect a constant, subtle awareness of constant Roman oppression. The critique was at times subtle, because they lived in the shadow of an empire and an overt call to revolt would lead to instant military response and annihilation for the Christian or Jewish communities. Theirs was a resistance of quiet faith and occasional actions of protest when they treated each other—slaves, women, poor, outcasts, and the lowly—with a dignity that the empire sought to deny them. We too often cannot hear their critique of the empire because we in the West are too far removed from their situation, our modern lives are too prosperous, and we live in so much freedom that their reality is beyond our ken. Were we to travel to many parts of our modern world, however, we would find people today who can read these texts and hear the message of silent, determined, subtle resistance to tyranny.

II

Having said this, I must confess that if you wish to discover a prophetic voice assaulting the prerogatives of kings, you need look no further than John the Baptist. He spoke against Herod Antipas, son of Herod the Great, and tetrarch of Galilee and Perea from 4 B.C.E. to 39

C.E. Herod married the former wife (or mother-in-law according to Josephus) of his deceased brother, Philip, who was named Herodias. As a Jew he could or even should marry the woman, if she had no sons, for that was the requirement of the Jewish Levirite law. But she did have a son, so the marriage was illicit by Jewish standards. John the Baptist criticized Herod for that and probably for the typical kind of economic oppression that client kings of the Romans so often wreaked upon their own people. Because of his prophetic indictment John lost his head to the machinations of Herodias and her dancing daughter (whom Josephus calls Salome; Mark 6:14-29; Matt 14:1-12; Luke 3:19-20; 9:7-9). Herodias manipulated Herod in the same way that Jezebel had power over Ahab, which then made John parallel with Elijah once again in keeping with his other symbolic gestures and lifestyle. But for our purposes it is worth noting how John the Baptist in his ministry went up against the power politics of his age and condemned a king.

III

If we wish to read a truly brutal story of how kings operate, we need look no further than the opening chapter of the Gospel of Matthew. We read the horrible account in Matt 2:16-18:

> [16]When Herod saw that he had been tricked by the wise men, he was infuriated, and he sent and killed all the children in and around Bethlehem who were two years old or under, according to the time that he had learned from the wise men. [17]Then was fulfilled what had been spoken through the prophet Jeremiah:
> [18]"A voice was heard in Ramah,
>   wailing and loud lamentation,
> Rachel weeping for her children;
>   she refused to be consoled, because they are no more."

Commentators often have commented that this brutal slaughter of little babies was typical of Herod, for he was the man who even put two of his sons and his wife to death because he thought they were plotting to seize the throne. Killing his sons prompted a Roman governor to quip that he would rather be Herod's pig than his son (that's because Jews don't eat pork, so Herod's pig would be safe—Roman humor). The commentators might better have said that not only was that brutal behavior of killing small children so typical of Herod, but it is typical of all kings.

In fact, it seems to be typical of too many rulers and warlords today. Tribal warlords in Africa use small children as soldiers in their armies, especially in contemporary Sudan and Somalia. How many genocides in Africa and Asia have involved the slaughter of small children as well as their families? Rwanda, Somalia, Sudan, Cambodia . . . . The list goes on. How many children died in the death camps in Nazi Germany? So much for civilized Christian nations! The list goes on! Herod was no exception; he was tragically too much of an archetype in human history, even today. We still have kings and tyrants. How many more Herods will walk across the pages of human history before it ends?

This tragic story has one good aspect to it. Herod was duped by the wise men. Though he wanted to kill Jesus, he failed in this task, because the wise men were warned by God in a dream not to return to Herod (Matt 2:12). So the all-powerful king failed as the wise men lived up to their reputation as wise men and went home by a different route than the king's palace. Once more a powerful and supposedly wise king was thwarted.

IV

Jesus addressed the issue of how his followers ought to relate to kings. The saying, "Render to Caesar the things that are Caesar's, and unto God the things that are God's," was recalled in Mark 12:17; Matt 22:21; and Luke 20:25. Though historically Christians have taken this as a straightforward imperative to divide up one's obligations appropriately between church and state, the original context of the saying by Jesus may have had negative overtones. In essence, Jesus may have been telling his disciples to give no more to the government, and Caesar, than the state deserved. God had to be put before Caesar, and given Jesus' assumption about how much of our life was owed to God and if indeed all aspects of life fell under the reign of God in the coming kingdom, perhaps very little of life was to be left for Caesar and other minions of that ilk. Jesus may have meant only that rebellion against Caesar should not be undertaken but that all other meaningful aspects of this life fell under the guidance of God.[3] "Jesus' words set a limit on the legitimacy of the state" for obedience Christians owed to those who were in authority.[4]

There was also some humor in this narrative. Some Herodians and Pharisees sought to trap Jesus with the question whether it was appropriate for Jews to pay taxes to Caesar. (Herodians were supporters of the various rulers named Herod, all of whom were enamored of Greek and Roman culture and ruled as puppet kings for the Roman Empire. These Herodians were Jewish representatives for the Roman Empire and perceived as traitors by many Jews.) Their question about taxes was a hot question for Jesus to handle. For if he said that Jews should pay taxes, then the poor peasant crowd that listened to Jesus would be alienated; but to declare that such taxes ought not be paid would brand Jesus as a revolutionary and lead to his immediate arrest and execution.

Jesus was clever. He asked for a coin. Quickly one of his critics produced a coin from his pocket, for his hand moved faster than his brain. Upon being asked whose picture was on the coin, he too quickly responded by saying it was Caesar's. Oops. He should not have let the crowd know that he possessed such a coin. For imperial coins circulated by the Roman Empire were impressed with images of the Graeco-Roman deities and pictures of the reigning emperor, which, of course, testified in some way to the divine status of that emperor. Thus, the coins had images of the gods and violated one of the Ten Commandments that said neither make nor own graven images of gods. Furthermore, the poor peasants who followed Jesus about were probably so poor as not to own such coins, for they traded with barter, not with coinage. The opponent of Jesus showed himself to be rich, at least in the minds of the peasant audience, and, even worse, an idolater who violated the command against graven images by flashing the coin in public and declaring the name of Caesar aloud. (I suppose, if you had to carry such coins, you should discreetly keep them in your pouch.) Immediately the crowd silently turned against Jesus' questioners. At this point Jesus answered the question with the definite edge in the confrontation. If the coin belonged to Caesar, and implicitly it should not even belong to a Jew, then return it to Caesar. Jesus gave an ambiguous answer. He did not directly say to pay taxes; he merely said that the accursed Roman coins should go back to the Romans. One could understand Jesus to be saying that we should return only to Caesar and his minions those evil things that belong to them, but everything else belonged to God. The saying would be a clever form of articulating passive resistance—give the empire no more than it deserved, and, of course, it really deserved nothing. The bottom line is that the saying was enmeshed in a clever story, which was essentially critical of the evil Roman Empire and Roman rulers especially. It was not straightforward discourse about the relationship of religious and secular authorities. Meanwhile, in the distance, we can see the

Herodians leaving the scene as one says to another, "I told you not to take that coin out of your pocket! Now let's get out of here before the crowd notices that we're leaving! We're lucky we weren't lynched!"

In other passages Jesus was quite critical of rulers and leaders of this age whose time is limited before the coming of the kingdom of God. Jesus also told his disciples not to lord it over each other as the rulers of this world did. In Mark 10:42-44 Jesus described the relationship Christians were to have, and he contrasted it with the way of kings and rulers:

> [42]You know that among the Gentiles those whom they recognize as their rulers lord it over them, and their great ones are tyrants over them. [43]But it is not so among you; but whoever wishes to become great among you must be your servant, [44]and whoever wishes to be first among you must be slave of all. (cf. Luke 22:24-27)

As with the Hebrew prophets, Jesus too maintained a critical stance against kings.

A humorous tale of healing by Jesus was recorded in Mark 5:1-20; Matt 8:28-34; and Luke 8:26-39. Jesus encountered a man possessed by many demons. As the demons were cast out, they identified themselves as "legion." They were cast into a herd or "troop" of swine, whereupon they immediately ran down a hill and drowned themselves. Of course, the Jewish audience found it humorous that a herd of pigs drowned themselves, since Jews did not think too highly of pork. But there might be deeper and darker humor here. "Legion" was a word used to describe Roman soldiers who carried out Caesar's orders to rule the Roman Empire. With that in mind one would further be tempted to think of the herd as a "troop" of soldiers and their rushing down the side of the hill as a military "charge." The image of drowning would bring to mind the drowning of Pharaoh's army in the sea (Exodus 15), which brought about the liberation of the ancient Israelites under Moses. The image of Roman "pig" soldiers drowning themselves in the sea, like Pharaoh's soldiers and chariots, might have come to mind for Jewish Christians as they told this story. They might have viewed the "legion" of demons who possessed the man to be like the Roman armies who "possessed" the Jewish people. If so, the story took a sarcastic potshot at Caesar and his lackeys.[5]

Jesus' entry into Jerusalem may have had a satirical side to it. Later Christians saw how Jesus imitated the procession of Davidic kings in Jerusalem after their coronation and thus implied that he was the expected Messiah (and thereby ensured his death by flaunting the Roman authorities in the Tower of Antonia overlooking his entry route). Jesus may have undertaken his ride in deliberate fulfillment of the expectation articulated in Zech 9:9 concerning the victorious king riding in on an ass. But there may have been more to Jesus' sense of prophetic and dramatic proclamation with his actions. In his day processions into cities were undertaken by Roman emperors and by ruling members of Herod's family in Palestine. Such processions were designed to impress upon the peasants the power and the grandeur of the particular ruler in the parade. By coming into Jerusalem dressed as a peasant and riding on a simple animal, Jesus made a strong statement about kings. True kings did not need to display wealth in such ostentatious fashion, but the shallow kings of that world flaunted their wealth and power in vainglorious parades designed to impress and intimidate the masses.

V

When later Christians spoke of Jesus as "Lord," they used an important political term taken from the language of that age. The Greek word, *kurios*, used by Christians to confess Jesus was also a political term used to describe the Roman emperor. It could be equated with the Latin title, Caesar. When Christians used the term for Jesus they stepped on the prerogatives of Roman emperors. When Christians said there was no other "lord" under heaven whereby people were saved, they defied the religious-political associations made with the Roman caesar, for Roman emperors wished to be viewed as divine and also as saviors of the people.[6] The Greek word for "savior," *soter*, was also a term used by Hellenistic kings in the Near East and Roman emperors, as well, to describe their roles in relation to the people whom they ruled. When Christians declared that these terms applied only to Jesus and no earthly ruler, they engaged in an act of civil disobedience by denying to the Roman emperors the honorific titles and adulation they demanded from their subjects. The refusal to call Caesar "lord" and pinch a bit of incense to burn in respect of his divinity was what earned many Christians a fast trip to the arena in those early centuries. To use the words *kurios* and *soter* for Jesus was a revolutionary act. Christians thus functioned indirectly as prophets condemning the arrogance of kings.

A number of other words and images might have been appropriated by the Christians in the rhetoric of "one-upmanship" over against Roman regal rhetoric. Caesar Augustus, and other caesars, not only claimed to be "lords" and "saviors" but also called on people to have "faith," *pistis*, in their leadership, and they were celebrated in urban centers by the "assemblies," *ekklesiai*, of leading people who acknowledged publicly their divine status. Christians had "faith" only in Jesus, and the "churches" or "assemblies" were an extension of the invisible "Body of Christ." The message of Caesar Augustus' rule and how he brought peace to the world was called the "good news," *euangelion*, which for Christians meant "the Gospel" of Jesus. Christians spoke of the second coming of Jesus as a "coming," *parousia*, which was also a term used to describe great political leaders, especially caesars, as they came to visit cities in the empire. In fact, authors loved to describe such royal "visits" to cities in rather grand fashion. Caesar Augustus also spoke of his divine birth augured by the presence of a star in the sky. There is quite a bit of coincidence here. One has to suspect that Christians stole the language of the Roman Empire and used it to describe their counter empire, the kingdom of God.[7]

When Christian authors began to write the gospels in the late first century, two authors, Matthew and Luke, crafted very cleverly written Infancy Narratives. Matthew 1–2 and Luke 1–2 contained much religious symbolism within the narratives. For our purposes, it is worth noting that the Infancy Narratives contained a veiled critical commentary on traditional understandings of kingship. Jesus was seen as the expected messiah, but he came as a meek and mild baby and not as a powerful lord born to purple silk in the palace. He was born to poor parents in a small town in poor conditions, and his birth was attended by foreigners—the Magi according to Matthew, and very poor and lowly shepherds according to Luke. Commentators discuss at length how the portrayal of his birth was designed to counter the royal propaganda of Rome that spoke of the great births of its caesars.

Caesar Augustus, whose real name was Octavian, ruled from 31 B.C.E. to 14 C.E., and he particularly propagandized the significance of his divine rule with powerful rhetoric. It began with his stepfather, Julius Caesar, who was said to be a "son of God" by virtue of his descent from the goddess Venus through her son Aeneas. Then Caesar Augustus built upon this image. He was accorded the title Caesar, which means "Lord" or "emperor," and, more significantly, the title "Augustus," which means the "divine one." He brought to an end a long period of Roman civil wars in 31 B.C.E., so he was heralded as the one who brought the great "age of peace." Coins and building inscriptions throughout his reign provided him with accolades such as "god," "lord," "savior of the world," "lord of the world," "god made manifest," and in Egypt he was titled the "god from god." We might note not only are these all titles for Jesus, but the "god made manifest" title reminds us of the language associated with the "epiphany" of Jesus, which later Christians connected to the coming of the wise men. Octavian was fathered supposedly by the god Apollo, who impregnated Octavian's mother, Atia. As this happened at night, Octavian's father had a dream wherein he saw the sun rise from his wife's womb. As a child Octavian had wondrous deeds associated with him. Inscriptions even spoke of the "good tidings" that Caesar Augustus brought to the world. We are clearly reminded of how the angels sang "good tidings" about the age of peace for all people to the shepherds to announce Jesus' birth and of how Jesus displayed wisdom to the teachers in the temple as a young boy—both stories are recorded in Luke 2. Needless to say, the successors of Caesar Augustus, after 14 C.E., attempted to claim all of this politico-theological language for themselves so as to unify the great Roman imperial rule under their own personal domination.[8] In return, Christians claimed the same things for their Lord and kept up a rather sturdy counterclaim for their kingdom of the poor and lowly.

Christians stole a great deal of political language from the imperial Roman propaganda machine. Jesus is the "son of God," "lord," "savior," "lord of the world," and all the other titles. Jesus had celestial beings sing "good tidings" at his humble birth. The age of peace brought by the babe of Bethlehem stood in dramatic contrast, however, to the Augustan Age brought by Rome, enforced by Roman armies, and imposed on peasant peoples with crushing force. The kingdom Jesus brought was for the poor, as clearly proclaimed by the songs in the Lukan narratives (the *Magnificat* and Simeon's song), and not for the rich and powerful of the Roman Imperium.[9] It is such a pity that the triumphalistic church over the years often has forgotten this early Christian rhetoric and those revolutionary beginnings that stressed the humble kingdom and rule of Jesus.

VI

Paul used the rhetoric of Roman politics to describe the new Christian movement, or the "Body of Christ" as he called it. As did other Christian thinkers in this era, so Paul also took the reigning political rhetoric (or propaganda) of the Roman Imperium and used it to describe the spiritual movement of Christians. Paul detested the cult of emperor worship, so he took the terminology of the emperors and their beneficence and applied it to Jesus and the mission of Christianity. Jesus was "lord" and "savior," not the caesars. The caesars proclaimed their "*euangelion*," or gospel, of imperial rule and its concomitant peace, justice, wealth, and unity, which was maintained by armies, economic power, building projects, bribery and flattery of the rich and powerful, political rhetoric, and oppression of the poor (with occasional crucifixions for dissidents and troublemakers). Paul, however, proclaimed a gospel of the weak and the poor who lived in the "Body of Christ." The *ekklesia*, the church, replaced the *polis*, the city-state; human weakness replaced human power as that which was deemed worthy in the eyes of God; imperial courts and public banquets in the Graeco-Roman cities were replaced by Christian communal religious meals, especially the eucharist; and ultimately the apocalyptic imagery of Paul and other New Testament authors condemned the so-called harmonious world order brought by the caesars. Paul proclaimed the message of Jesus, who was a victim of imperial corruption brutally executed in the manner reserved for slaves, revolutionaries, and foreigners. Paul sought to convert both Jews and Gentiles to a movement of spiritual liberation by countering the "theology of empire" with the "theology of the crucified one."[10]

Some Christians today might appeal to Paul's discourse in Rom 13:1-7 about obedience to the authorities as an indication that Paul was not as critical of the government as Hebrew prophets had been. Christians have oft appealed to this passage when they condemn civil disobedience by Christians in our modern age or call for a very respectful response of Christians to their government. But that kind of reading fails to appreciate the sarcasm behind Paul's observations. He called for obedience, observing that the authorities were a terror to those who were evil (vv. 3-4), and he recommended paying taxes and giving respect. But we know that Paul also expected Jesus to bring the world to an end, and those very same Roman authorities would be the target of judgment and punishment on that day. Paul, like other Christians, probably recognized that until that time when God would judge the evil rulers of this world, those rulers at least prevented chaos in the world, and that was beneficial to the spread of Christianity.[11]

We must not forget that Paul was a Jew who could recall quite readily the brutal repression visited upon Jews by the Romans even prior to the Jewish revolt (66–70 C.E.). Paul proclaimed the victory of Jesus over death, and Jesus was a victim of Roman rule put to death by Roman soldiers and a handful of Jewish collaborators. He spoke not only of spiritual wickedness but also of imperial Roman corruption and oppression when he referred to "this present evil age" (Gal 1:4), "a crooked and perverse generation" (Phil 2:15), an age that is "passing away" (1 Cor 7:31), an age under divine wrath (1 Thess 1:10; Rom 5:9).[12] All of these expressions countered Roman propaganda about the age of peace and prosperity brought by the empire. These characterizations aptly described the corrupt political, personal, and sexual activities of the various caesars, especially Caligula and Nero.

Paul probably believed that Christians should work with the government in the same way that they were to love their enemies also—not because government leaders were good, but because loving them might win some of them for Christ! We must not forget that the emperor at the time Paul wrote Romans was Nero, and he probably viewed Nero as a tyrant, though he did not say it directly.[13] Nor should we forget that his letter was written to people in Rome, who lived under the very nose of that emperor. Paul had not seen this people; this letter was his "letter of introduction" to them. Paul, of course, was politically astute about what he said in this letter, and he did not encourage his listeners to engage in foolish actions that would lead to their own self-destruction. Not too long before this letter was written, some Jews were expelled from Rome, perhaps because of controversies concerning the teachings of Jesus. Were his letter to fall into the wrong hands, his Roman Christian audience would suffer greatly. The ultimate irony of his advice in Romans 13 was that Paul was addressing people who had been oppressed by Rome and would ultimately be martyred by Rome. His was not the theology of political accommodation, this was the theology of a martyr, who knew that God would avenge the deaths of the innocent.[14] His form of resistance to Rome was to create a community of poor, marginal, and oppressed people who worshiped a victim executed by the empire in a movement that gave them dignity and a sense of equality. Thus, we must be careful in using this passage in Romans too strongly in our discourse about Paul's understanding of the relationship of Christians to those in authority or the modern ethical question of the Christian's obedient relationship to contemporary governments.

VII

Though the New Testament literature was primarily interested in proclaiming the message and actions of Jesus, especially the universal significance of his death and resurrection for the salvation of all people, nonetheless, we still encounter significant images of prophetic critique of kings and emperors. This is impressive, since the authors assumed the imminent return of Jesus and therefore did not feel constrained to address social and political issues as directly as did the Hebrew prophets. If all people stood before God as equals by virtue of their sinfulness and subsequent redemption by Jesus, then distinctions between the ruled and the rulers are inconsequential. Nowhere was this stated better than by Paul in Gal 3:28, "There is no longer Jew or Greek, there is no longer slave or free, there is no longer male and female; for all of you are one in Christ Jesus." In time this concept would help translate into one of the many babbling brooks that would flow into the river of democratic thought.

Conclusion

For many centuries Christians accepted the rule of kings and even spoke of the divine right by which they ruled. Christians also accepted slavery until the nineteenth century, not realizing that their monotheistic faith demanded abolition of this brutal institution long before that time. In part, a society has to be ready for revolutionary thought to transform itself into common social praxis. European and American society would not be ready to realize and actualize the biblical critique of kings and class systems until the last few centuries. Even more important, the radical concepts found within the biblical texts had to be made available for reading to a wider range of Christian believers, and this would take the invention of the printing press and the willingness of educated Christians to translate the Bible into the vernacular languages so that many more might read it. Such conditions did not exist until the sixteenth century and beyond.

Along the way there were Christian visionaries who sensed the radical implications of the prophetic message and the teachings of Jesus and Paul in the New Testament. There would be religious orders that would forsake the political and economic structures of this world to create a more humble and just society of their own. There would be Christian theologians, mystics, and other reflective thinkers who would sense that the ultimate implication of the biblical message was a society free from kings, classes, and economic oppression. But too often they could not obtain a hearing from the Christian masses, and their insights were lost in the crushing onward flow of history. Though they might be canonized as saints occasionally, their beliefs were often regarded as too idealistic for the practical everyday world. Sometimes a two-kingdom theory would safely relegate their vision of society to an ideal Christian utopian vision, the ideal life of the church, or a reality to be fulfilled only in the afterlife, while the real world was to function with the hard, practical ethics of old—ethics hardly changed from the time when pagans ruled the world. At those times when idealistic visionaries tried to create egalitarian societies—peasants' movements in the Middle Ages, Hussites and Anabaptists in the early modern period, and so many other Christian experiments—they were silenced by the sharp sword of the "Christian" civil authorities, Catholic and Protestant, who saw them as a threat to social order. Only in the modern era have the Christian idealists bequeathed their legacy of equality to actual social-political entities, the modern democratic states. But from the very beginning such entities were destined to be the outcome of the monotheistic (r)evolution.

Throughout the biblical tradition there was a disdain for powerful autocrats and those who used power to oppress the poor and weak. The biblical assumptions of equality before God reinforced this rhetoric, for implicit in this notion of equality was the implication that perhaps there should not be kings or leaders who by some dint were considered to be superior or closer to the divine realm than those subjects whom they ruled. It was that very assumption of the divinity of the ruler that was most directly attacked by a monotheistic religion, for that religion assumed equality before the one God and could brook no arrogance of a human being who dared appeal to God in order to vaunt himself over other human beings.

We can still speak of an evolution or an unfolding of these ideals in Western society. It would require more than a millennium and a half before Western European society could hear the fuller implications of this biblical message, but eventually the biblical values would unfold more dramatically in the emergence of democratic thought. Beginning in the early modern period, with the Reformation and beyond, theologians and subsequently political thinkers would quote biblical texts along with other texts to articulate their understandings of the rights of humanity and the basic equality of all humanity. The biblical text would be used to strike a blow for human equality, freedom, and dignity more effectively by secular spokespersons and more frequently than by representations of ecclesial institutions (though some church representatives did add their voices to the chorus). "In its secularized form the Christian ethos still has been unfolding, in recent centuries, in the form of modern democratic ideals."[1] Hopefully, as that process continues, more spokespersons within the ecclesial institutions will see that the biblical message and hence the ecclesiastical message should resonate with those secular

voices, begotten by the Judeo-Christian movement, that cry for the end
of tyranny and kingship in all its manifestations and the beginning of
human freedom, equality, and dignity.

We live in an era wherein we have more power to address the political
abuses in our society and continue the ages-long movement toward
democratic justice in society and great human equality. When the ancients heard the critique of kings in the biblical text, they could yearn
for God to act. When we hear the stories we must realize that the burden
now falls on us to correct the problems in our society. Too often people
complain about why God lets something bad happen. Maybe the real
answer is that God is waiting for people to do something to correct situa-
tions in which bad things happen. After all, are we not made in the image
of God with a rational mind and a human conscience? Were we not told
in Genesis 1 to rule the world wisely? Instead of complaining about why
bad things happen, maybe we are being called by God to do something.
If we read these biblical accounts and hear the abrasive critique about
kings, tyranny, and the abuse of human rights, and then if we see a connection between those stories and events happening today, maybe we
should do something about it, especially beginning with our regular
periodic revolution at the ballot box. Daniel Berrigan said it well:

> And what of ourselves, the governed? We too dwell in moral dark-
> ness, deep and often unapprehended; we who approve such rulers
> or are prudently silent in the face of their crimes. We who offer, in
> our secret longings, small relief from theirs. Tendencies in leader
> and follower are often alike, and hold firm; self-interest, ego, lust,
> greed, duplicity, the common mire from which spring the wily and
> witless among us.[2]

Abbreviations

AB	Anchor Bible
ABD	*Anchor Bible Dictionary*, 6 vols., ed. David Noel Freedman
ASORDS	American Schools of Oriental Research Dissertation Series
ATANT	Abhundlungen zur Theologie des Alten und Neuen Testaments
BA	*Biblical Archaeologist*
BTB	*Biblical Theology Bulletin*
BZAW	Beihefte zur Zeitschrift für die alttestamentliche Wissenschaft
CBC	Cambridge Bible Commentary
CBQ	*Catholic Biblical Quarterly*
Herm	Hermeneia
FRLANT	Forschungen zur Religion und Literatur des Alten und Neuen Testaments
IB	*Interpreter's Bible*, 12 vols., ed. George Buttrick
ICC	International Critical Commentary
Int	*Interpretation*
JBL	*Journal of Biblical Literature*
JSOT	*Journal for the Study of the Old Testament*
JSOTSup	Journal for the Study of the Old Testament Supplement Series
NCBC	New Cambridge Bible Commentary
OBT	Overtures to Biblical Theology
OTL	Old Testament Library
Sem	Semeia
SBLMS	Society of Biblical Literature Monograph Series

SWBA	Social World of Biblical Antiquity
VT	*Vetus Testamentum*
WBC	Word Biblical Commentary
WMANT	Wissenschaftliche Monographien zum Alten und Neuen Testament
WTJ	*Westminster Theological Journal*
ZAW	*Zeitschrift für die alttestamentliche Wissenschaft*

Notes

Chapter 1, pages 1–13

1. Henri Frankfort, *Kingship and the Gods: A Study of Ancient Near Eastern Religion as the Integration of Society and Nature* (Chicago, IL: University of Chicago Press, 1948); Cyril Gadd, *Ideas of Divine Rule in the Ancient Near East* (Oxford, Eng.: Oxford University Press, 1948); Roland de Vaux, *Ancient Israel: Its Life and Institutions*, trans. John McHugh (New York: McGraw-Hill, 1961), 100–144; Robert Gnuse, "Kingship in the Ancient World" (Thesis, Christ Seminary-Seminex, St. Louis, 1974); Madeleine and Lane Miller, *Harper's Encyclopedia of Bible Life*, 3rd ed. (San Francisco, CA: Harper & Row, 1978), 252–58; and Keith Whitelam, *The Just King*, JSOTSup 12 (Sheffield, Eng: JSOT Press, 1979).

2. Dale Launderville, *Piety and Politics: The Dynamics of Royal Authority in Homeric Greece, Biblical Israel, and Old Babylonian Mesopotamia* (Grand Rapids, MI: Eerdmans, 2003).

3. Benson Bobrick, *Wide as the Waters: The Story of the English Bible and the Revolution It Inspired* (New York: Simon and Schuster, 2001), 278–84.

4. Ibid., 267–97.

5. Henning Graf Reventlow, *The Authority of the Bible and the Rise of the Modern World*, trans. John Bowden (Philadelphia: Fortress, 1985), 413 et passim.

6. Jack Lewis, "Versions, English (Pre-1960): Wycliffe's Version," *ABD* 6:830.

7. Norman Cohn, *The Pursuit of the Millennium*, rev. ed. (New York: Oxford University Press, 1970), 205–22.

8. Donald Lutz, *The Origins of American Constitutionalism* (Baton Rouge, LA: Louisiana State Univ., 1988), 7, 25, 60–61; and *A Preface to American Political Theory* (Lawrence, KS: University of Kansas, 1992), 69, 115.

9. Lutz, "The Relative Influence of European Writers on Late Eighteenth-Century American Political Thought," *The American Political Science Review* 78 (1984): 192; and *Constitutionalism*, 44, 67, 87, 114, 118, 130, 140–42, 169; and *Political Theory*, 121, 135–37.

Lutz maintains that today we do not recognize sufficiently the implications attested to by this statistical difference, *Political Theory*, 136.

10. Lutz, *Political Theory*, 116, 136; and George Connor, "Covenants and Criticisms: Deuteronomy and the American Founding," *BTB* 32 (2002): 4–10, who notes the striking social, political, and economic parallels between the time of Josiah, when the book of Deuteronomy arose, and the colonial period.

11. Thomas Paine, *Rights of Man, Common Sense, and Other Political Writings* (New York: Oxford University Press, 1995), 12–13; Richard Ketchum, *The Winter Soldiers: The Battles for Trenton and Princeton* (New York: Doubleday, 1991), 9; and Edward Davidson and William Scheick, *Paine, Scripture, and Authority* (London and Toronto: Associated University Presses, 1994), 29.

12. Ketchum, *Winter Soldiers*, 9.

13. Baruch Halpern, *David's Secret Demons: Messiah, Murderer, Traitor, King* (Grand Rapids, MI: Eerdmans, 2001).

14. Stephen McKenzie, *King David: A Biography* (New York: Oxford University Press, 2000).

15. Stuart Lasine, *Knowing Kings: Knowledge, Power, and Narcissism in the Hebrew Bible* (Atlanta, GA: Society of Biblical Literature, 2001).

16. Robert Alter, *The David Story: A Translation with Commentary of 1 and 2 Samuel* (New York: Norton, 1999).

17. Jung Ju Kang, *The Persuasive Portrayal of Solomon in 1 Kings 1–11* (New York: Peter Lang, 2003), 141–302.

18. J. G. McConville, *God and Earthly Power: An Old Testament Political Theology: Genesis–Kings* (New York: T & T Clark, 2006).

19. David Lamb, *Righteous Jehu and His Evil Heirs: The Deuteronomist's Negative Perspective on Dynastic Succession*, Oxford Theological Monographs. Vol. 10 (New York: Oxford University Press, 2007).

20. Douglas Knight, "Political Rights and Powers in Monarchic Israel," *Sem* 66 (1994): 93–117.

21. Eckart Otto, "Of Aims and Methods in Hebrew Bible Ethics," *Sem* 66 (1994): 162.

22. Walter Brueggemann, *The Prophetic Imagination* (Philadelphia, PA: Fortress, 1978); and James Walsh, *The Mighty from Their Thrones*, OBT (Philadelphia, PA: Fortress, 1987).

23. George Mendenhall, *The Tenth Generation* (Baltimore, MD: Johns Hopkins University Press, 1973); George Pixley, *God's Kingdom*, trans. Donald Walsh (Maryknoll, NY: Orbis, 1981); Norman Gottwald, *The Tribes of Yahweh* (Maryknoll, NY: Orbis, 1979); and many essays by these and other scholars. Cf. Bruce Birch, *Let Justice Roll Down* (Louisville, KY: Westminster John Knox, 1991), uses the categories in less heavy-handed fashion than the others, and this typifies a more modified contemporary approach.

24. David Jamieson-Drake, *Scribes and Schools in Monarchic Judah*, JSOTSup, vol. 190 and SWBA, vol. 9 (Sheffield, Eng.: JSOT Press, 1991).

25. Otto, "Aims," 165; and Anne Fitzpatrick-McKinley, *The Transformation of Torah from Scribal Advice to Law*, JSOTSup, vol. 287 (Sheffield, Eng.: Sheffield Academic Press, 1999).

Chapter 2, pages 14–26

1. G. M. Crowfoot, *Early Ivories from Samaria* (London: Palestine Exploration Fund, 1938); and Shalom Paul, *Amos*, Herm (Philadelphia, PA: Fortress, 1991), 126.

2. James Mays, *Amos*, OTL (Philadelphia, PA: Westminster, 1969), 71.

3. William Harper, *Amos and Hosea*, ICC (Edinburgh: T & T Clark, 1905), 86; Hans Walter Wolff, *Joel and Amos*, trans. Waldemar Janzen, Dean McBride, and Charles Muenchow, Herm (Philadelphia, PA: Fortress, 1977), 205–6; and Paul, *Amos*, 128–29.

4. Mays, *Amos*, 116.

5. Wolff, *Joel and Amos*, 276.

6. Mays, *Hosea*, OTL (Philadelphia, PA: Westminster, 1969), 80.

7. Harper, *Amos and Hosea*, 295.

8. Hans Walter Wolff, *Hosea*, trans. Gary Stansell, Herm (Philadelphia, PA: Fortress, 1974), 124.

9. Harper, *Amos and Hosea*, 297; and Francis Andersen and David Noel Freedman, *Hosea* (Garden City, NY: Doubleday, 1980), 447–48.

10. Wolff, *Hosea*, 139.

11. Harper, *Amos and Hosea*, 314–15; and Andersen and Freedman, *Hosea*, 492.

12. Wolff, *Hosea*, 227.

13. Otto Kaiser, *Isaiah 1–12*, trans. R. A. Wilson, OTL (Philadelphia, PA: Westminster, 1972), 128–30.

14. Dale Launderville, *Piety and Politics*, 300. Cf. Ronald Clements, *Isaiah 1–39*, NCBC (Grand Rapids, MI: Eerdmans, 1980), 122.

15. Mays, *Micah*, OTL (Philadelphia, PA: Westminster, 1976), 77.

16. Delbert Hillers, *Micah*, Herm (Philadelphia, PA: Fortress, 1984), 66.

Chapter 3, pages 27–38

1. John Carroll, *Jeremiah*, OTL (Philadelphia, PA: Westminster, 1986), 412.

2. Ibid., 642.

3. John Bright, *Jeremiah* (Garden City, NY: Doubleday, 1965), 182.

4. Walther Zimmerli, *Ezekiel 2*, trans. James Martin, Herm (Philadelphia, PA: Fortress, 1983), 213.

5. G. A. Cooke, *Ezekiel*, ICC (Edinburgh: T & T Clark, 1936), 131; Walther Eichrodt, *Ezekiel*, trans. Cosslett Quinn, OTL (Philadelphia, PA: Westminster, 1970), 150–51; and Zimmerli, *Ezekiel 1*, trans. Ronald Clements, Herm (Philadelphia, PA: Fortress, 1979), 267–74.

6. Eichrodt, *Ezekiel*, 390; and Zimmerli, *Ezekiel 2*, 77–80.

7. Eichrodt, *Ezekiel*, 391.

8. Ibid., 425; and Zimmerli, *Ezekiel 2*, 146–47.

9. Eichrodt, *Ezekiel*, 432.

10. George Buchanan Gray, *Isaiah*, ICC (Edinburgh: T & T Clark, 1912), 255.

11. William Dever, "How Was Ancient Israel Different?" in *The Breakout: The Origins of Civilization*, ed. Martha Lamberg-Karlovsky (Cambridge, MA: Harvard University Press, 2000), 65.

Chapter 4, pages 39–46

1. Donald Gowan, *Theology in Exodus: Biblical Theology in the Form of a Commentary* (Louisville, KY: Westminster John Knox, 1994), 180.

2. Cf. Millard Lind, *Yahweh Is a Warrior: Theology of Warfare in Ancient Israel* (Scottdale, PA: Herald Press, 1980), 64 et passim.

3. George Ernest Wright, "Deuteronomy," *IB* 2:441–43; Gerhard von Rad, *Deuteronomy*, trans. Dorothea Barton, OTL (Philadelphia, PA: Westminster, 1966), 118–20; and Anthony Phillips, *Deuteronomy*, CBC (Cambridge, Eng.: Cambridge University Press, 1973), 120–22, all stress particularly the revolutionary nature of this legislation.

4. Norbert Lohfink, "Distribution of the Functions of Power: The Laws Concerning Public Offices in Deuteronomy 16.18–18.22," in *A Song of Power and the Power of Song: Essays on the Book of Deuteronomy*, Sources for Biblical and Theological Study, ed. Duane Christensen (Winona Lake, IN: Eisenbrauns, 1993), 336–52; and Launderville, *Piety and Politics*, 323–24.

5. Gary Knoppers, "Rethinking the Relationship between Deuteronomy and the Deuteronomistic History: The Case of Kings," *CBQ* 63 (2001): 401–2.

6. Lind, *Yahweh Is a Warrior*, 151.

7. John Rogerson, *Chronicle of the Old Testament Kings* (London, Eng.: Thames and Hudson, 1999), 72.

8. Richard Lowery, *The Reforming King*, JSOTSup, vol. 120 (Sheffield, Eng.: JSOT Press, 1990), 153–57.

9. Knoppers, "Rethinking the Relationship," 397–402, but Knoppers' overall argument is that the books of Kings portrays Solomon's wealth and power in such a positive light, that the book of Kings stands in tension with Deuteronomy by not condemning the prerogatives of royal power (393–415).

10. McConville, "Singular Address in the Deuteronomic Law and the Politics of Legal Administration," JSOT 97 (2002): 19–36.

11. Eckart Otto, "False Weights in the Scales of Biblical Justice," in *Gender and Law in the Hebrew Bible and the Ancient Near East*, ed. Victor Matthews, et al., JSOTSup, vol. 262 (Sheffield, Eng.: Sheffield, 1998), 145.

12. Stephen Orgel and Jonathan Goldberg, eds., *John Milton: The Major Works*, Oxford World Classics (Oxford, Eng.: Oxford University Press, 2003), 350–53, cited in McConville, *God and Earthly Power*, 175.

13. McBride, "Polity of the Covenant People: The Book of Deuteronomy," *Int* 41 (1987): 243.

Chapter 5, pages 47–65

1. Gnuse, "Redefining the Elohist," *JBL* 119 (2000): 201–20.

2. Alan Jenks, *The Elohist and North Israelite Traditions*, SBLMS, vol. 22 (Missoula, MT: Scholars Press, 1977).

3. Gnuse, *No Other Gods: Emergent Monotheism in Israel*, JSOTSup, vol. 241 (Sheffield, Eng.: Sheffield Academic Press, 1997).

4. Martin Noth, *Exodus*, trans. John Bowden (Philadelphia, PA: Westminster, 1962), 23–24; and John Durham, *Exodus*, WBC (Waco, TX: Word, 1987), 11.

5. Terence Fretheim, *Exodus*, Interpretation (Louisville, KY: John Knox Press, 1991), 31–32.

6. Ibid., 34.

7. Brevard Childs, *The Book of Exodus*, OTL (Philadelphia, PA: Westminster, 1974), 11.

8. Brian Lewis, *The Sargon Legend* and, ASORDS, vol. 4 (Cambridge, MA: American Schools of Oriental Research, 1980); and Rainer Kessler, "The Threefold Image of Egypt in the Hebrew Bible," *Scriptura* 90 (2005): 881.

9. Gary Rendsburg, "Moses as Equal to Pharaoh," *Text, Artifact, and Image: Revealing Ancient Israelite Religion*, ed. Gary Beckman and Theodore Lewis, Brown Judaic Studies, vol. 346 (Providence, RI: Brown University, 2006), 201–19.

10. Durham, *Exodus*, 15.

11. Lind, *Yahweh Is a Warrior*, 61–62.

12. Fretheim, *Exodus*, 35.

13. McConville, *God and Earthly Power*, 28.

14. Rendsburg, "Moses as Equal to Pharaoh," 201–4.

15. Gowan, *Theology in Exodus*, 135–36.

16. José Miranda, *Marx and the Bible: A Critique of the Philosophy of Oppression*, trans. John Eagleson (Maryknoll, NY: Orbis, 1974), 78–88.

17. William Propp, *Exodus 1–18*, AB (Garden City, NY: Doubleday, 1998), 530–31, 554–59.

18. Lind, *Yahweh Is a Warrior*, 53–59; and Gerald Janzen, *Exodus*, Westminster Bible Companion (Louisville, KY: Westminster John Knox, 1997), 105–7.

19. David Pleins, *The Social Visions of the Hebrew Bible: A Theological Introduction* (Louisville, KY: John Knox Press, 2001), 162.

Chapter 6, pages 66–76

1. Richard Nelson, *The Double Redaction of the Deuteronomistic History*, JSOTSup vol. 18 (Sheffield, Eng.: JSOT Press, 1981).

2. Rudolf Smend, "Das Gesetz und die Völker: Ein Beitrag zur deuteronomistischen Redaktionsgeschichte," *Probleme biblischer Theologie*, ed. Hans Walter Wolff (Munich: Beck, 1971), 494–509, whose ideas were developed by Walter Dietrich, *Prophetie und Geschichte*, FRLANT, vol. 108 (Göttingen: Vandenhoeck & Ruprecht, 1972).

3. Iain Provan, *Hezekiah and the Book of Kings*, BZAW, vol. 172 (New York: Walter de Gruyter, 1998); and Marvin Sweeney, *I & II Kings*, OTL (Louisville, KY: Westminster John Knox, 2007), 4–26.

4. Birch, *Let Justice Roll Down* (Louisville, KY: Westminster John Knox, 1991), 206.

5. Lind, *Yahweh Is a Warrior*, 69, 79–82.

6. Martin Buber, *Kingship of God*, 3rd ed., trans. Richard Scheimann (New York, NY: Harper and Row, 1967), 69.

7. Cristiano Grottanelli, "The Enemy King Is a Monster: A Biblical Equation," *Kings and Prophets: Monarchic Power, Inspired Leadership, and Sacred Text in Biblical Narrative* (New York: Oxford University Press, 1999), 51–52.

8. Buber, *Kingship*, 70.

9. Dennis Olsen, "Buber, Kingship, and the Book of Judges: A Study of Judges 6–9 and 17–21," in *David and Zion: Biblical Studies in Honor of J. J. M. Roberts*, eds. Bernard Batto and Kathryn Roberts (Winona Lake, IN: Eisenbrauns, 1994), 199–218; and McConville, *God and Earthly Power*, 129.

10. Reinhard Müller, *Königtum und Gottesherrschaft: Untersuchungen zur alttestamentlichen Monarchiekritik*, Forschungen zum Alten Testament 2. Reihe, vol. 3 (Tübingen: Mohr Siebeck, 2004), 12.

11. Buber, *Kingship*, 75.

12. Müller, *Königtum*, 26.

Chapter 7, pages 77–93

1. Walsh, *The Mighty from Their Thrones*, 89–95.

2. Birch, *Let Justice Roll Down*, 210.

3. Paine, *Rights of Man*, 13–14; Ketchum, *Winter Soldiers*, 9; and Davidson and Scheick, *Paine, Scripture, and Authority*, 29.

4. Alter, *The David Story*, 62.

5. Grottanelli, "The Enemy King Is a Monster," 63.

6. Ibid., 53.

7. Ibid., 51–69, esp. 69.

8. Alter, *The David Story*, 139.

9. Donald Murray, *Divine Prerogative and Royal Pretension*, JSOTSup, vol. 264 (Sheffield, Eng.: Sheffield Academic Press, 1998), 252–63.

10. Alter, *The David Story*, 293.

11. David Gunn, *The Story of King David: Genre and Interpretation* (Sheffield, Eng.: JSOT Press, 1978), 95.

12. Jacob Klein, "Akitu," *ABD* 1:138–40; and "Sacred Marriage," *ABD* 5:866–70.

13. Bruce Power, "'All the King's Horses . . .': Narrative Subversion in the Story of Solomon's Golden Age," in *From Babel to Babylon: Essays on Biblical History and Literature in Honour of Brian Peckham*, ed. Joyce Wood, John Harvey, and Mark Leuchter, JSOTSup, vol. 455 (New York: T & T Clark, 2006), 112–13.

14. Lasine, *Knowing Kings*, 115–16.

15. Sweeny, *I & II Kings*, 61.

16. Power, "All the King's Horses," 111–23.

17. Sweeney, *I & II Kings*, 63.

18. Lasine, *Knowing Kings*, 148.

19. Sweeney, *I & II Kings*, 89.

20. Birch, *Let Justice Roll Down*, 222.

Chapter 8, pages 94–105

1. Gnuse, *No Other Gods*, 186–87; and Wesley Toews, *Monarchy and Religious Institutions in Israel under Jeroboam I*, SBLMS, vol. 47 (Atlanta, GA: Scholars Press, 1993).

2. Simon DeVries, *1 Kings*, WBC (Waco, TX: Word, 1985), 172; and Andersen and Freedman, *Amos*, AB (Garden City, NY: Doubleday, 1989), 842.

3. Davie Napier, "The Inheritance and the Problem of Adjacency," *Int* 39 (1976): 3–11; and Gnuse, *You Shall Not Steal: Community and Property in the Biblical Tradition* (Maryknoll, NY: Orbis, 1984), 74–75. Nadav Naʾaman, "Naboth's Vineyard and the Foundation of Jezreel," JSOT 33 (2008): 197–218, suggests that this story is recalled by the biblical author because it typifies what Ahab did repeatedly to small landowners when he built the royal city of Jezreel, and his strong-arm tactics were not forgotten.

4. Patrick Cronauer, *The Stories about Naboth the Jezreelite: A Source, Composition, and Redaction Investigation of 1 Kings 21 and Passages in 2 Kings 9* (New York: T & T Clark, 2005), 113–204.

5. Maxwell Miller, "The Elisha Cycle and the Accounts of the Omride Wars," *JBL* 85 (1966): 441–54; Herbert Donner, "The Separate States of Israel and Judah," in *Israelite and Judean History*, ed. John Hayes and Maxwell Miller, OTL (Philadelphia, PA: Westminster, 1977), 399–400; and Sweeney, *I & II Kings*, 238–39, 255–57.

6. Grottanelli, "Religious Ideals and the Distribution of Cereal Grains in the Hebrew Bible," *Kings and Prophets*, 38.

7. Sweeney, *I & II Kings*, 311.

8. Napier, "The Omrides of Jezreel," *VT* 9 (1959): 366–78; Horst Seebass, "Der Fall Naboth in 1 Reg XXI," *VT* 24 (1974): 474–88; Gnuse, *Steal*, 74–75; and Walsh, *Mighty from their Thrones*, 105–7.

9. Dever, "Ancient Israel Different," 62–67.

10. Lind, *Yahweh Is a Warrior*, 173.

11. McConville, *God and Earthly Power*, 155.

12. Lasine, *Knowing Kings*, 163.

Chapter 9, pages 106–18

1. John Van Seters, *Abraham in History and Tradition* (New Haven, CT: Yale University, 1975); *Abraham, In Search of History* (New Haven, CT: Yale University Press, 1983); *Prologue to History* (Louisville, KY: Westminster John Knox, 1992); and *Life of Moses* (Louisville, KY: Westminster John Knox, 1994); Hans Heinrich Schmid, *Der Sogenannte Jahwist* (Zürich: Theologische Verlag, 1976); Rolf Rendtorff, *Das Ubelieferungsgeschichtliche Problem des Pentateuch*, BZAW, vol. 147 (Berlin: Walter de Gruyter, 1977); Norman Whybray, *The Making of the Pentateuch* , JSOTSup, vol. 53 (Sheffield, Eng.: Sheffield Academic Press, 1987), 43–131. Joseph Blenkinsopp, *The Pentateuch* (New York: Doubleday, 1992) suggests that the Priestly narrative is prior to the Yahwist. Some scholars prefer to limit the "Primeval History" to Genesis 1–9, maintaining that Genesis 10–11 belongs to the Patriarchal Narratives as a prehistory, Bernard Batto, *Slaying the Dragon* (Louisville, KY: Westminster John Knox, 1992), 69; and Theodore Hiebert, *The Yahwist's*

Landscape: Nature and Religion in Early Israel (New York: Oxford University Press, 1996), 80–82.

2. Johnson Lim, *Grace in the Midst of Judgment: Grappling with Genesis 1–11*, BZAW, vol. 314 (New York, NY: Walter de Gruyter, 2002).

3. Bobrick, *Wide as the Waters*, 60; and Cohn, *Pursuit of the Millennium*, 199.

4. Bobrick, *Wide as the Waters*, 59–62; and Alastair Dunn, *The Great Rising of 1381* (Charleston, SC: Tempus, 2002), 59–62, 140.

5. Mark Smith, *The Origins of Biblical Monotheism: Israel's Polytheistic Background and the Ugaritic Texts* (New York: Oxford University Press, 2001), 169.

6. David Silverman, "Divinity and Deities in Ancient Israel," *Religion in Ancient Egypt: Gods, Myths, and Personal Practice*, ed. Byron Shafer (Ithaca, NY: Cornell University Press, 1991), 66.

7. Batto, "The Divine Sovereign: The Image of God in the Priestly Creation Account," *David and Zion*, ed. Batto and Roberts, 179.

8. Ibid., 182.

9. Ibid., 185.

10. Lind, *Yahweh Is a Warrior*, 124.

11. Batto, "The Divine Sovereign," 183–85.

12. Ibid., 169–71.

13. Bruce Vawter, *On Genesis* (Garden City, NY: Doubleday, 1970), 55–60; Claus Westermann, *Genesis 1–11*, trans. John Scullion (Minneapolis, MN: Augsburg, 1984), 151–61; and Karl Löning and Erich Zenger, *To Begin With, God Created . . . : Biblical Theologies of Creation*, trans. by Omar Kaste (Collegeville, MN: Liturgical Press/Glazier Press, 2000), 108–11.

14. Abraham Malamat, "Mari," *BA* 34 (1971): 7; and Lind, *Yahweh Is a Warrior*, 125.

15. Brueggemann, "From Dust to Kingship," *ZAW* 84 (1972): 1–18; and Nicolas Wyatt, "Interpreting the Creation and Fall Story in Genesis 2–3," *ZAW* 93 (1981): 10–21.

16. Vawter, *Genesis*, 74.

17. Lind, *Yahweh Is a Warrior*, 123.

18. A. Leo Oppenheim, "Sumerian King List," *Ancient Near Eastern Texts Relating to the Old Testament*, 3rd ed., ed. James Pritchard (Princeton, NJ: Princeton University Press, 1970), 265–66.

19. Lind, *Yahweh Is a Warrior*, 122.

20. Richard Hess, "Enoch," *ABD* 2:508.

21. M. Smith, *The Early History of God: Yahweh and the Other Deities in Ancient Israel* (San Francisco, CA: Harper and Row, 1990), 115–34; and Glen Taylor, *Yahweh and the Sun*, JSOTSup, vol. 111 (Sheffield, Eng.: Sheffield Academic Press, 1993).

22. M. G. Kline, "Divine Kingship and Genesis 6:1-4," *WTJ* 24 (1962): 187–210; and David Clines, "Theme in Genesis 1–11," *CBQ* 38 (1976): 495; *The Theme of the Pentateuch*, JSOTSup, vol. 10 (Sheffield, Eng.: University of Sheffield Press, 1978), 69–70; and "The Significance of the 'Sons of God' Episode (Genesis 6:1-4) in the Context of the 'Primeval History' (Genesis 1–11)," *JSOT* 13 (1979): 33–46.

23. Van Seters, *The Life of Moses*, 182–84; and Daniel Smith-Christopher, *A Biblical Theology of Exile*, OBT (Minneapolis, MN: Fortress, 2002), 67.

24. Smith-Christopher, *Biblical Theology of Exile*, 67.

Chapter 10, pages 119–28

1. Norman Porteous, *Daniel*, OTL (Philadelphia, PA: Westminster, 1965), 67–68.

2. Ibid., 65–73; and Sibley Towner, *Daniel*, Interpretation (Atlanta, GA: John Knox, 1984), 67–68.

3. John Goldingay, *Daniel*, WBC (Dallas, TX: Word, 1989), 94.

4. André Lacocque, *The Book of Daniel*, trans. David Pellauer (Atlanta, GA: John Knox, 1979), 76; and Towner, *Daniel*, 65.

5. Porteous, *Daniel*, 59.

6. Goldingay, *Daniel*, 73–74.

7. Porteous, *Daniel*, 76.

8. Towner, *Daniel*, 71–72.

9. Lacocque, *Daniel*, 92, 101.

10. John Gammie, *Daniel*, Knox Preaching Guides (Atlanta, GA: Jon Knox, 1983), 57–58.

11. Lacocque, *Daniel*, 112; and Towner, *Daniel*, 81.

12. Carey Moore, *Daniel, Esther and Jeremiah: The Additions*, AB (Garden City, NY: Doubleday, 1977), 117–25.

13. Moore, *Esther*, AB (Garden City, NY: Doubleday, 1971), 13–14; and Jon Levenson, *Esther*, OTL (Louisville, KY: Westminster John Knox, 1997), 12–14.

14. Levenson, *Esther*, 12.

15. Ibid., 13.

16. Michael Fox, *Character and Ideology in the Book of Esther* (Columbia, SC: University of South Carolina Press, 1991), 173.

17. Sandra Beth Berg, *The Book of Esther*, SBLDS, vol. 44 (Missoula, MT: Scholars Press, 1979), 62–69; and Levenson, *Esther*, 98.

18. Levenson, *Esther*, 14.

19. Bernard Bailyn, *The Ideological Origins of the American Revolution* (Cambridge, MA: Belknap Press, 1967), 126–27.

20. Moore, *Judith*, AB (Garden City, NY: Doubleday, 1985), 67–71.

21. Toni Craven, *Artistry and Faith in the Book of Judith*, SBLDS, vol. 70 (Chico, CA: Scholars Press, 1983), 2.

Chapter 11, pages 129–40

1. Gnuse, "Contemporary Evolutionary Theory as a New Heuristic Model for the Social Scientific Method in Biblical Studies," *Zygon* 25 (1990): 405–31.

2. Richard Horsley and Neil Asher Silberman, *The Message and the Kingdom: How Jesus and Paul Ignited a Revolution and Transformed the Ancient World* (Minneapolis, MN: Fortress, 1997), 2.

3. Floyd Filson, *A Commentary on the Gospel according to St. Matthew* (New York: Harper and Row, 1960), 235; Dennis Nineham, *St. Mark*, Pelican Gospel Commentaries (Baltimore, MD: Penguin, 1963), 316; Larry Hurtado, *Mark* (San Francisco, CA: Harper and Row, 1983), 181; Lamar Williamson, *Mark*, Interpretation (Atlanta, GA: John Knox, 1983), 219–21; Duncan Derrett, "Luke's Perspective on Tribute to Caesar," in *Political Issues in Luke-Acts*, ed. Richard Cassidy and Philip Scharper (Maryknoll,

NY: Orbis, 1983), 38–48; and Horsley and Silberman, *Message and the Kingdom*, 83–84; Horsley, *Jesus and Empire: The Kingdom of God and the New World Disorder* (Minneapolis, MN: Fortress, 2003), 99.

4. Hurtado, *Mark*, 181.

5. Horsley, *Jesus and Empire*, 100–101, 108.

6. N. T. Wright, "Paul's Gospel and Caesar's Empire," in *Paul and Politics: Ekklesia, Israel, Imperium, Interpretation*, ed. Horsley (Harrisburg, PA: Trinity, 2000), 168–69.

7. Horsley, *Jesus and Empire*, 133–34.

8. John Dominic Crossan and Jonathan Reed, *In Search of Paul* (San Francisco, CA: HarperSanFrancisco, 2004), 235–36; and Marcus Borg, *Jesus: Uncovering the Life, Teachings, and Relevance of a Religious Revolutionary* (New York: HarperOne, 2006), 66–68.

9. Horsley, *The Liberation of Christmas: The Infancy Narratives in Social Context* (New York: Crossroad, 1989), 1–172.

10. Neil Elliott, *Liberating Paul: The Justice of God and the Politics of the Apostle* (Maryknoll, NY: Orbis, 1994), 93–230; and the various essays in Horsley, ed., *Paul and Politics*, especially Elliott, "Paul and the Politics of Empire," 17–39; Horsley, "Rhetoric and Empire—and 1 Corinthians," 72–102; and Wright, "Paul's Gospel," 160–83.

11. C. K. Barrett, *A Commentary on the Epistle to the Romans* (New York: Harper and Row, 1957), 244–49; William Barclay, *The Letter to the Romans*, rev. ed. (Philadelphia, PA: Westminster, 1975), 173–74; and Paul Achtemeier, *Romans*, Interpretation (Atlanta, GA: John Knox, 1985), 203–7.

12. Elliott, *Liberating Paul*, 93–230, especially 98. Elliott also suggests that even Paul's criticisms of sexual deviance may be commentary on the escapades of the caesars and their powerful political minions more than they are meant to be a statement about general sexual morality for the masses (193–95).

13. Ernst Käsemann, *Commentary on Romans*, trans. Geoffrey Bromiley (Grand Rapids, MI: Eerdmans, 1980), 356.

14. Elliott, *Liberating Paul*, 217–26.

Conclusion, pages 141–43

1. Karl Luckert, *Egyptian Light and Hebrew Fire* (Albany, NY: SUNY Press, 1991), 289.

2. Daniel Berrigan, *The Kings and Their Gods: The Pathology of Power* (Grand Rapids, MI: Eerdmans, 2008), 3.

Bibliography

Achtemeier, Paul. *Romans*. Interpretation. Atlanta, GA: John Knox, 1985.

Alter, Robert. *The David Story: A Translation with Commentary of 1 and 2 Samuel*. New York: Norton, 1999.

Andersen, Francis, and David Noel Freedman. *Amos*. AB. Garden City, NY: Doubleday, 1989.

————. *Hosea*. AB. Garden City, NY: Doubleday, 1980.

Bailyn, Bernard. *The Ideological Origins of the American Revolution*. Cambridge, MA: Belknap Press, 1967.

Barclay, William. *The Letter to the Romans*. Rev. ed. Philadelphia, PA: Westminster, 1975.

Barrett, C. K. *A Commentary on the Epistle to the Romans*. New York: Harper and Row, 1957.

Batto, Bernard. "The Divine Sovereign: The Image of God in the Priestly Creation Account." In *David and Zion: Biblical Studies in Honor of J. J. M. Roberts*, edited by Bernard Batto and Kathryn Roberts, 143–86. Winona Lake, IN: Eisenbrauns, 2004.

————. *Slaying the Dragon*. Louisville, KY: Westminster John Knox, 1992.

Berg, Sandra Beth. *The Book of Esther*. SBLDS. Vol. 44. Missoula, MT: Scholars Press, 1979.

Berrigan, Daniel. *The Kings and Their Gods: The Pathology of Power*. Grand Rapids, MI: Eerdmans, 2008.

Birch, Bruce. *Let Justice Roll Down*. Louisville, NY: Westminster John Knox, 1991.

Blenkinsopp, Joseph. *The Pentateuch*. New York: Doubleday, 1992.

Bobrick, Benson. *Wide as the Waters: The Story of the English Bible and the Revolution It Inspired*. New York: Simon and Schuster, 2001.

Borg, Marcus. *Jesus: Uncovering the Life, Teachings, and Relevance of a Religious Revolutionary*. New York: HarperOne, 2006.

Brueggemann, Walter. "From Dust to Kingship." *ZAW* 84 (1972): 1–18.

————. *The Prophetic Imagination*. Philadelphia, PA: Fortress, 1978.

Buber, Martin. *Kingship of God*. Translated by Richard Scheimann. 3rd ed. New York: Harper and Row, 1967.

Carroll, John. *Jeremiah*. OTL. Philadelphia, PA: Westminster, 1986.

Childs, Brevard. *The Book of Exodus*. OTL. Philadelphia, PA: Westminster, 1974.

Clements, Ronald. *Isaiah 1–39*. NCBC. Grand Rapids, MI: Eerdmans, 1980.

Clines, David. "The Significance of the 'Sons of God' Episode (Genesis 6:1-4) in the Context of the 'Primeval History' (Genesis 1–11)." *JSOT* 13 (1979): 33–46.

———. "Theme in Genesis 1–11," *CBQ* 38 (1976): 483–507.

———. *The Theme of the Pentateuch*. JSOTSup. Vol. 10. Sheffield, Eng.: University of Sheffield Press, 1978.

Cohn, Norman. *The Pursuit of the Millennium*. Rev. ed. New York: Oxford University Press, 1970.

Connor, George. "Covenants and Criticisms: Deuteronomy and the American Founding." *BTB* 32 (2002): 4–10.

Cooke, G. A. *Ezekiel*. ICC. Edinburgh: T & T Clark, 1936.

Craven, Toni. *Artistry and Faith in the Book of Judith*. SBLDS. Vol. 70. Chico, CA: Scholars Press, 1983.

Cronauer, Patrick. *The Stories about Naboth the Jezreelite: A Source, Composition, and Redaction Investigation of 1 Kings 21 and Passages in 2 Kings 9*. New York: T & T Clark, 2005.

Crossan, John Dominic, and Jonathan Reed. *In Search of Paul*. San Francisco, CA: HarperSanFrancisco, 2004.

Crowfoot, G. M. *Early Ivories from Samaria*. London, Eng.: Palestine Exploration Fund, 1938.

Davidson, Edward, and William Scheick. *Paine, Scripture, and Authority*. London and Toronto: Associated University Presses, 1994.

Derrett, Duncan. "Luke's Perspective on Tribute to Caesar." In *Political Issues in Luke-Acts*, edited by Richard Cassidy and Philip Scharper, 38–48. Maryknoll, NY: Orbis, 1983.

Dever, William. "How Was Ancient Israel Different?" In *The Breakout: The Origins of Civilization*, edited Martha Lamberg-Karlovsky, 62–67. Cambridge, MA: Harvard University Press, 2000.

DeVries, Simon. *1 Kings*. WBC. Waco, TX: Word, 1985.

Dietrich, Walter. *Prophetie und Geschichte*. FRLANT. Vol. 108. Göttingen: Vandenhoeck & Ruprecht, 1972.

Donner, Herbert. "The Separate States of Israel and Judah." In *Israelite and Judean History*, edited by John Hayes and Maxwell Miller, 381–434. OTL. Philadelphia, PA: Westminster, 1977.

Dunn, Alastair. *The Great Rising of 1381*. Charleston, SC: Tempus, 2002.

Durham, John. *Exodus*. WBC. Waco, TX: Word, 1987.

Eichrodt, Walther. *Ezekiel*. Translated by Cosslett Quinn. OTL. Philadelphia, PA: Westminster, 1970.

Elliott, Neil. *Liberating Paul: The Justice of God and the Politics of the Apostle*. Maryknoll, NY: Orbis, 1994.

———. "Paul and the Politics of Empire." In *Paul and Politics: Ekklesia, Israel, Imperium, Interpretation*, edited by Richard Horsley, 17–39. Harrisburg, PA: Trinity, 2000.

Filson, Floyd. *A Commentary on the Gospel according to St. Matthew*. New York: Harper and Row, 1960.

Fitzpatrick-McKinley, Anne. *The Transformation of Torah from Scribal Advice to Law*. JSOTSup. Vol. 287. Sheffield, Eng.: Sheffield, 1999.

Fox, Michael. *Character and Ideology in the Book of Esther*. Columbia, SC: University of South Carolina Press, 1991.

Frankfort, Henri. *Kingship and the Gods*. Chicago, IL: University of Chicago Press, 1948.

Fretheim, Terence. *Exodus*. Interpretation. Louisville, KY: John Knox Press, 1991.

Gnuse, Robert. "Kingship in the Ancient World." Thesis, Christ Seminary-Seminex, St. Louis, 1974.

———. *No Other Gods: Emergent Monotheism in Israel*. JSOTSup. Vol. 241. Sheffield, Eng.: Sheffield Academic Press, 1997.

———. "Redefining the Elohist." *JBL* 119 (2000): 201–20.

———. *You Shall Not Steal: Community and Property in the Biblical Tradition*. Maryknoll, NY: Orbis, 1984.

Goldingay, John. *Daniel*. WBC. Dallas, TX: Word, 1989.

Gottwald, Norman. *The Tribes of Yahweh*. Maryknoll, NY: Orbis, 1979.

Gowan, Donald. *Theology in Exodus: Biblical Theology in the Form of a Commentary*. Louisville, KY: Westminster John Knox, 1994.

Gray, George Buchanan. *Isaiah*. ICC. Edinburgh: T & T Clark, 1912.

Grottanelli, Cristiano. *Kings and Prophets: Monarchic Power, Inspired Leadership, and Sacred Text in Biblical Narrative*. New York: Oxford University Press, 1999.

———. "The Enemy King Is a Monster: A Biblical Equation." In *Kings and Prophets*, 47–72.

———. "Religious Ideals and the Distribution of Cereal Grains in the Hebrew Bible." In *Kings and Prophets*, 31–45.

Gunn, David. *The Story of King David: Genre and Interpretation*. Sheffield, Eng.: JSOT Press, 1978.

Halpern, Baruch. *David's Secret Demons: Messiah, Murderer, Traitor, King*. Grand Rapids, MI: Eerdmans, 2001.

Harper, William. *Amos and Hosea*. ICC. Edinburgh: T & T Clark, 1905.

Hess, Richard. "Enoch." *ABD* 2:508.

Hiebert, Theodore. *The Yahwist's Landscape: Nature and Religion in Early Israel*. New York: Oxford University, 1996.

Hillers, Delbert. *Micah*. Herm. Philadelphia, PA: Fortress, 1984.

Horsley, Richard. *Jesus and Empire: The Kingdom of God and the New World Disorder*. Minneapolis, MN: Fortress, 2003.

———. *The Liberation of Christmas: The Infancy Narratives in Social Context*. New York: Crossroads, 1989.

———, ed. *Paul and Politics: Ekklesia, Israel, Imperium, Interpretation*. Harrisburg, PA: Trinity, 2000.

———. "Rhetoric and Empire—and 1 Corinthians." In *Paul and Politics*, edited by Richard Horsley, 72–102.

———, and Neil Asher Silberman. *The Message and the Kingdom: How Jesus and Paul Ignited a Revolution and Transformed the Ancient World*. Minneapolis, MN: Fortress, 1997.

Hurtado, Larry. *Mark*. San Francisco, CA: Harper and Row, 1983.

Jamieson-Drake, David W. *Scribes and Schools in Monarchic Judah*. JSOTSup. Vol. 190. SWBA. Vol. 9. Sheffield, Eng.: JSOT Press, 1991.

Janzen, Gerald. *Exodus*. Westminster Bible Companion. Louisville, KY: Westminster John Knox, 1997.

Jenks, Alan. *The Elohist and North Israelite Traditions*. SBLMS. Vol. 22. Missoula, MT: Scholars Press, 1977.

Kaiser, Otto. *Isaiah 1–12*. Translated by R. A. Wilson. OTL. Philadelphia, PA: Westminster, 1972.

Kang, Jung Ju. *The Persuasive Portrayal of Solomon in 1 Kings 1–11*. New York: Peter Land, 2003.

Käsemann, Ernst. *Commentary on Romans*. Translated by Geoffrey Bromiley. Grand Rapids, MI: Eerdmans, 1980.

Kessler, Rainer. "The Threefold Image of Egypt in the Hebrew Bible." *Scriptura* 90 (2005): 878–84.

Ketchum, Richard. *The Winter Soldiers: The Battles for Trenton and Princeton*. New York: Doubleday, 1991.

Klein, Jacob. "Akitu." *ABD* 1:138–40.

———. "Sacred Marriage." *ABD* 5:866–70.

Kline, M. G. "Divine Kingship and Genesis 6:1-4." *WTJ* 24 (1962): 187–210.

Knight, Douglas. "Political Rights and Powers in Monarchic Israel." *Sem* 66 (1994): 93–117.

Knoppers, Gary. "Rethinking the Relationship between Deuteronomy and the Deuteronomistic History: The Case of Kings." *CBQ* 63 (2001): 393–415.

Lacocque, André. *The Book of Daniel*. Translated by David Pellauer. Atlanta, GA: John Knox, 1979.

Lamb, David. *Righteous Jehu and His Evil Heirs: The Deuteronomist's Negative Perspective on Dynastic Succession*. Oxford Theological Monographs. Vol. 10. New York: Oxford University Press, 2007.

Lasine, Stuart. *Knowing Kings: Knowledge, Power, and Narcissism in the Hebrew Bible*. Atlanta, GA: Society of Biblical Literature, 2001.

Launderville, Dale. *Piety and Politics: The Dynamics of Royal Authority in Homeric Greece, Biblical Israel, and Old Babylonian Mesopotamia.* Grand Rapids, MI: Eerdmans, 2003.

Levenson, Jon. *Esther.* OTL. Louisville, KY: Westminster John Knox, 1997.

Lewis, Brian. *The Sargon Legend.* ASORDS. Vol. 4. Cambridge, MA: American Schools of Oriental Research, 1980.

Lewis, Jack. "Versions, English (Pre-1960): Wycliffe's Version." *ABD* 6:830.

Lim, Johnson. *Grace in the Midst of Judgment: Grappling with Genesis 1–11.* BZAW. Vol. 314. New York: Walter de Gruyter, 2002.

Lind, Millard. *Yahweh Is a Warrior: Theology of Warfare in Ancient Israel.* Scottdale, PA: Herald Press, 1980.

Lohfink, Norbert. "Distribution of the Functions of Power: The Laws Concerning Public Offices in Deuteronomy 16.18–18.22." In *A Song of Power and the Power of Song: Essays on the Book of Deuteronomy,* edited by Duane Christensen, 336–52. Sources for Biblical and Theological Study. Winona Lake, IN: Eisenbrauns, 1993.

Löning, Karl, and Erich Zenger. *To Begin With, God Created . . . : Biblical Theologies of Creation.* Translated by Omar Kaste. Collegeville, MN: Liturgical Press/Glazier Press, 2000.

Lowery, Richard. *The Reforming King.* JSOTSup. Vol. 120. Sheffield, Eng.: JSOT Press, 1990.

Luckert, Karl. *Egyptian Light and Hebrew Fire.* Albany: SUNY Press, 1991.

Lutz, Donald. *The Origins of American Constitutionalism.* Baton Rouge, LA: Louisiana State University Press, 1988.

———. *A Preface to American Political Theory.* Lawrence, KS: University of Kansas Press, 1992.

———. "The Relative Influence of European Writers on Late Eighteenth-Century American Political Thought." *The American Political Science Review* 78 (1984): 189–97.

Malamat, Abraham. "Mari." *BA* 34 (1971).

Mays, James. *Amos.* OTL. Philadelphia, PA: Westminster, 1969.

———. *Hosea.* OTL. Philadelphia, PA: Westminster, 1969.

———. *Micah.* OTL. Philadelphia, PA: Westminster, 1976.

McBride, Dean. "Polity of the Covenant People: The Book of Deuteronomy." *Int* 41 (1987): 229–44.

McConville, J. G. *God and Earthly Power: An Old Testament Political Theology: Genesis-Kings.* Library of Hebrew Bible/Old Testament Studies. Vol. 454. New York: T & T Clark, 2006.

———. "Singular Address in the Deuteronomic Law and the Politics of Legal Administration." *JSOT* 97 (2002): 19–36.

McKenzie, Stephen. *King David: A Biography.* New York: Oxford University Press, 2000.

Mendenhall, George. *The Tenth Generation*. Baltimore, MD: Johns Hopkins University Press, 1973.

Miller, Madeleine, and Lane Miller. *Harper's Encyclopedia of Bible Life*. 3rd ed. San Francisco, CA: Harper & Row, 1978.

Miller, Maxwell. "The Elisha Cycle and the Accounts of the Omride Wars." *JBL* 85 (1966): 441–54.

Miranda, José. *Marx and the Bible: A Critique of the Philosophy of Oppression*. Translated by John Eagleson. Maryknoll, NY: Orbis, 1974.

Moore, Carey. *Daniel, Esther and Jeremiah: The Additions*. AB. Garden City, NY: Doubleday, 1977.

———. *Esther*. AB. Garden City, NY: Doubleday, 1971.

———. *Judith*. AB. Garden City, NY: Doubleday, 1985.

Müller, Reinhard. *Königtum und Gottesherrschaft: Untersuchungen zur alttestamentlichen Monarchiekritik*. Forschungen zum Alten Testament 2. Reihe. Vol. 3. Tübingen: Mohr Siebeck, 2004.

Murray, Donald. *Divine Prerogative and Royal Pretension*. JSOTSup. Vol. 264. Sheffield, Eng.: Sheffield Academic Press, 1998.

Naʾaman, Nadav. "Naboth's Vineyard and the Foundation of Jezreel." *JSOT* 33 (2008): 197–218.

Napier, Davie. "The Inheritance and the Problem of Adjacency." *Int* 39 (1976): 3–11.

———. "The Omrides of Jezreel." *VT* 9 (1959): 366–78.

Nelson, Richard. *The Double Redaction of the Deuteronomistic History*. JSOTSup. Vol. 18. Sheffield, Eng.: JSOT Press, 1981.

Nineham, Dennis. *St. Mark*. Pelican Gospel Commentaries. Baltimore, MD: Penguin, 1963.

Noth, Martin. *Exodus*. Translated by John Bowden. Philadelphia: Westminster, 1962.

Olsen, Dennis. "Buber, Kingship, and the Book of Judges: A study of Judges 6–9 and 17–21." In *David and Zion: Biblical Studies in Honor of J. J. M. Roberts*, edited by Bernard Batto and Kathryn Roberts, 199–218. Winona Lake, IN: Eisenbrauns, 1994.

Oppenheim, A. Leo. "Sumerian King List." In *Ancient Near Eastern Texts Relating to the Old Testament*. edited by James Pritchard, 265–66. 3rd ed. (Princeton, NJ: Princeton University, 1970.

Otto, Eckart. "False Weights in the Scales of Biblical Justice." In *Gender and Law in the Hebrew Bible and the Ancient Near East*, edited by Victor Matthews, et al., 128–46. JSOTSup. Vol. 262. Sheffield, Eng.: Sheffield, 1998.

———. "Of Aims and Methods in Hebrew Bible Ethics." *Sem* 66 (1994): 161–72.

Paine, Thomas. *Rights of Man, Common Sense, and Other Political Writings*. New York: Oxford University Press, 1995.

Paul, Shalom. *Amos*. Herm. Philadelphia, PA: Fortress, 1991.

Phillips, Anthony. *Deuteronomy*. CBC. Cambridge, Eng.: Cambridge University Press, 1973.

Pixley, George. *God's Kingdom*. Translated by Donald Walsh. Maryknoll, NY: Orbis, 1981.

Pleins, David. *The Social Visions of the Hebrew Bible: A Theological Introduction*. Louisville, KY: John Knox Press, 2001.

Porteous, Norman. *Daniel*. OTL. Philadelphia, PA: Westminster, 1965.

Power, Bruce. "'All the King's Horses . . .': Narrative Subversion in the Story of Solomon's Golden Age." In *From Babel to Babylon: Essays on Biblical History and Literature in Honour of Brian Peckham*, edited by Joyce Wood, John Harvey, and Mark Leuchter, 111–23. JSOTSup. Vol. 455. New York: T & T Clark, 2006.

Propp, William. *Exodus 1–18*. AB. Garden City, NY: Doubleday, 1998.

Provan, Iain. *Hezekiah and the Book of Kings*. BZAW. Vol. 172. New York: Walter de Gruyter, 1998.

von Rad, Gerhard. *Deuteronomy*. OTL. Translated by Dorothea Barton. Philadelphia, PA: Westminster, 1966.

Rendsburg, Gary. "Moses as Equal to Pharaoh." In *Text, Artifact, and Image: Revealing Ancient Israelite Religion*, edited by Gary Beckman and Theodore Lewis, 201–19. Brown Judaic Studies. Vol. 346. Providence, RI: Brown University, 2006.

Rendtorff, Rolf. *Das Ubelieferungsgeschichtliche Problem des Pentateuch*, BZAW. Vol. 147. Berlin: Walter de Gruyter, 1977.

Reventlow, Henning Graf. *The Authority of the Bible and the Rise of the Modern World*. Translated by John Bowden. Philadelphia, PA: Fortress, 1985.

Rogerson, John. *Chronicle of the Old Testament Kings*. London, Eng.: Thames and Hudson, 1999.

Schmid, Han Heinrich. *Der Sogenannte Jahwist,*. Zürich: Theologische Verlag, 1976.

Seebass, Horst. "Der Fall Naboth in 1 Reg XXI." *VT* 24 (1974): 474–88.

Silverman, David. "Divinity and Deities in Ancient Israel." In *Religion in Ancient Egypt: Gods, Myths, and Personal Practice*, edited by Byron Shafer, 7–87. Ithaca, NY: Cornell University Press, 1991.

Smend, Rudolph. "Das Gesetz und die Völker: Ein Beitrag zur deuteronomistischen Redaktionsgeschichte." In *Probleme biblischer Theologie*, edited by Hans Walter Wolff, 494–509. Munich: Beck, 1971.

Smith, Mark. *The Early History of God: Yahweh and the Other Deities in Ancient Israel*. San Francisco, CA: Harper and Row, 1990.

———. *The Origins of Biblical Monotheism: Israel's Polytheistic Background and the Ugaritic Texts*. New York: Oxford University Press, 2001.

Smith-Christopher, Daniel. *A Biblical Theology of Exile*. OBT. Minneapolis, MN: Fortress, 2002.

Sweeney, Marvin. *I & II Kings*. OTL. Louisville, KY: Westminster John Knox, 2007.

Taylor, Glen. *Yahweh and the Sun*, JSOTSup. Vol. 111. Sheffield, Eng.: Sheffield, 1993.

Toews, Wesley. *Monarchy and Religious Institutions in Israel under Jeroboam*. SBLMS. Vol. 47. Atlanta, GA: Scholars Press, 1993.

Towner, Sibley. *Daniel*. Interpretation. Atlanta, GA: John Knox, 1984.

Van Seters, John. *Abraham in History and Tradition*. New Haven, CT: Yale University, 1975.

———. *Abraham, In Search of History*. New Haven, CT: Yale University, 1983.

———. *Life of Moses*. Louisville, KY: Westminster John Knox, 1994.

———. *Prologue to History*. Louisville, KY: Westminster John Knox, 1992.

de Vaux, Roland. *Ancient Israel: Its Life and Institutions*. Translated by John McHugh. New York: McGraw-Hill, 1961.

Vawter, Bruce. *On Genesis*. Garden City, NY: Doubleday, 1970.

Walsh, James. *The Mighty from Their Thrones*. OBT. Philadelphia: Fortress, 1987.

Westermann, Claus. *Genesis 1–11*. Translated by John Scullion. Minneapolis, MN: Augsburg, 1984.

Whitelam, Keith. *The Just King*. JSOTSup 12. Sheffield, Eng.: JSOT Press, 1979.

Whybray, Norman. *The Making of the Pentateuch*. JSOTSup. Vol. 53. Sheffield, Eng.: Sheffield Academic Press, 1987.

Williamson, Lamar. *Mark*. Interpretation. Atlanta: John Knox, 1983.

Wolff, Hans Walter. *Hosea*. Translated by Gary Stansell. Herm. Philadelphia, PA: Fortress, 1974.

———. *Joel and Amos*. Translated by Waldemar Janzen, Dean McBride, and Charles Muenchow. Herm. Philadelphia, PA: Fortress, 1977.

Wright, George Ernest. "Deuteronomy." *IB* 2:441–43.

Wright, N. T. "Paul's Gospel and Caesar's Empire." In *Paul and Politics: Ekklesia, Israel, Imperium, Interpretation*, ed. Richard Horsley, 160–83. Harrisburg, PA: Trinity, 2000.

Wyatt, Nicolas. "Interpreting the Creation and Fall Story in Genesis 2–3." *ZAW* 93 (1981): 10–21.

Zimmerli, Walther. *Ezekiel 1*. Translated by Ronald Clements. Herm. Philadelphia, PA: Fortress, 1979.

———. *Ezekiel 2*. Translated by James Martin. Herm. Philadelphia, PA: Fortress, 1983.

Index of Persons and Subjects

Scripture Index